LISTEN WITH THE EAR OF THE HEART

NÓIRÍN NÍ RIAIN

Listen with the Ear of the Heart
An Autobiography

VERITAS

Published 2009 by
Veritas Publications
7–8 Lower Abbey Street,
Dublin 1, Ireland

publications@veritas.ie
www.veritas.ie

ISBN 978-1-84730-172-7

Copyright © Nóirín Ní Riain, 2009

10 9 8 7 6 5 4 3 2 1

'God permits industrious Angels' by Emily Dickinson taken from *The Complete Poems of Emily Dickinson*, edited by Thomas H. Johnson, courtesy of Faber and Faber, 1970. Lines from 'Burnt Norton' by T.S. Eliot taken from *The Complete Poems and Plays of T.S. Eliot*, courtesy of Faber and Faber, 1969. Lines from 'Station Island' by Seamus Heaney, taken from *Station Island*, courtesy of Faber and Faber, 1984. Lines from 'When you are old' and 'Tom O'Roughley' by William Butler Yeats, by permission of AP Watt on behalf of Gráinne Yeats. Lines from 'The Musician' by R.S. Thomas, taken from *The Faber Book of Religious Verse*, courtesy of Faber and Faber, 1972.

Reproduction of St John the Theologian, original icon based on xvith century prototype from the Vatopedi Monastery of Mt Athos. Egg tempera on board (2000), courtesy of Fearghal O'Farrell.

A catalogue record for this book is available from the British Library.

Designed by Lir Mac Cárthaigh
Printed in Ireland by ColourBooks Ltd, Dublin

Veritas books are printed on paper made from the wood pulp of managed forests. For every tree felled, at least one tree is planted, thereby renewing natural resources.

DEDICATION

This book is dedicated to my first cousin, Carmel Sheridan, whose constant presence in my life continues to strengthen, support and keep the ear of my heart safe.

Many's the time as children we harmonised together the familiar strains of 'Whispering Hope', taught to us by our two 'aunty nuns', and we still do, thank God!

Soft as the voice of an angel,
Breathing a lesson unheard ...
Whispering hope, oh how welcome thy voice,
Making my heart in its sorrow rejoice.

Contents

~

SECOND MOVEMENT:
NOURISHING THE EAR OF THE HEART

~

'Listen ... and Incline the Ear of Your Heart'

LISTEN' IS THE VERY FIRST WORD OF St Benedict's Rule for the monastic life. He echoed the Sacred Scriptures, which he probably would have learned 'off by heart': 'Hear, O Heavens, and listen, O earth' – the opening advice of the first prophet Isaiah. Benedict says: 'Listen ... and incline the ear of your heart.' It is something that holds a lot of wisdom for us all in our lives.

In 2003, I wrote up a doctorate on a theology of listening. The primary purpose of such a thesis was to contribute to theological discourse. In other words, it had to be objective, impartial and detached, so I could not draw on personal stories of the Sound of God. The word 'I' could only be seen in footnotes.

Afterwards, everyone around me said, 'How very interesting, but we want to hear your story now. What was it that drove you to the precipice of expression? What is the history behind the text? How did you come to an awareness of "theosony", the Sound of God?' Hence, this book is an attempt to answer these three questions, a wedding of the 'I' and the ear between the covers.

There are moments in our lives when we are startled into reality by a sound, a word, or indeed a silence.

This sometimes gentle, sometimes raucous sound whispers to us a sudden recognition of our own belonging in this strange world, and we become deafened with a truth beyond the horizons of our everyday lives. When I seized the opportunity of defining my experience of a listening God, I immediately felt that a new word would have to appear to cover the myriad concepts that listening to, and out for, God embraces. Of course, the realm of silence is the other side of the hearing coin. So there is listening to God with the ear of the heart, the Word of God, the Voice of God, the Silence of God.

And so it came to be that a little word, 'theosony', became a welcome guest late in my life. It is a blend of two words from two different languages: 'Theos' is the lovely word for 'God' in Greek, which has been the source of many familiar words like 'theology', basically God-talk; 'theopathy', simply the emotion of just thinking about God; or 'theophany', plainly the appearance of God to humanity; and 'sonans' from the Latin, meaning 'sounding'. So 'theosony' modestly attempts to rope in all chatter, emotional conversation and dialogue, all listening, aural and silent appearances when our human heart rests in the divine heart.

It has been a daunting task to sculpt my own story – the personal story, the social story, the story of the sound of God. In the instances of lonesomeness in my life, listening out for the voice of the Divine was nearer to me than any other way of being. God is omnipresent, the aural icon of the silent Divine. The ear of the heart is the religious imagination of all desire and is simply yet another symbol of the Holy Spirit, the Supreme Goddess of Sound and Silence, the vital energy behind every sound where everyone, including the profoundly deaf, has a unique aural love affair with God. 'The Spirit blows ... and you hear the sound of it' (John 3:8); so it is with everyone who desires to know and live out a life of belonging and meaning with God. The ear of my heart has always cried out for God's quiet voice. It is our host to that realm of the stranger.

This book is one attempt to offer new insights and truths based on the narrative of some of my own aural and oral relationship with the triune God. I became ready to write and my tongue was 'the pen of a ready scribe' (Psalm 45:1). My story falls into three different movements of contrasting moods and feelings. The musical composition of a sonata (closely related to the Latin word '*sonans*') accurately symbolises my journey with its distinctive themes – sometimes happy, sometimes sad, but all near relatives in pitch and tune along the way. Therefore, I have adopted this musical scaffolding, topped with this introductory overture and tailed with a little coda, to tell the tale. My hope for it is that it may resonate with you, find the blessing that a sure 'sound' hue of listening can offer; that it may open your ears to hear the healing that such a blessing can bring. Hearing and listening with the ear of the heart is wholesome and holistic; we desperately need to cherish the aural in our noisy, troubled world. My own experiences, although sometimes clumsily articulated, are my attempt to share some brief vignettes or small sound-bytes of when I was audibly touched. May we all learn to listen that we may live. Let our hearing hearts incline to listen with the heavenly hosts, the communion of Saints, to the sonorous, deeply resonant song of salvation.

13

FIRST MOVEMENT
Growing in Sound

First Memories that Linger

I WAS CONCEIVED BESIDE THE OLDEST SACRED site in Ireland – the ancient stone circle near the beautiful Lough Gur, Co. Limerick. The family home was a tiny rented cottage on the banks of that magical lake, and I lived there with my parents, older sister and brother from the day of my birth, on 12 June 1951, until the age of four. I have no conscious memories of this time, although those stones, just standing there in silence for over four thousand years, are forever calling me back. Early childhood prepared me for a life committed first to God, and then to song. I had no idea until I revisited the shadowy hearth of my memories that this divine commitment was to be my space of ease, healing and homeliness.

My parents, Nora Hassett and Paddy Ryan, met in 1938. It was love at first sight, and for many years they were seen as the local 'golden couple'. He was the handsome creamery manager – a highly sought-after position in those days – and she was the stylish 'national' school teacher.

In 1955, the Marian year, we moved down the road to Caherconlish, into a fine newly built, two-storey house that had to be called Mount Marian. Years later my mother told me that on that first day in our new home, I was cranky and cross with a severe ear infection. Her mother had to be summoned to mind me in the midst of the unpacking. A moment sitting on Granny's lap in the bare front dining room is one of my earliest memories. Faintly I hear her singing softly to me. My right ear throbs when I recall it.

But my strongest memory of Mount Marian remains the sound of the clocks. The rhythmic ticking of the oak-framed clock over the Aga cooker punctuated the day as regularly as the numerous calls to prayer of Glenstal Abbey were to do so years later. And then there was the eccentric cuckoo clock in the living room, a gift that Da had brought back from a business trip to Holland. Although the little timber cuckoo didn't look or sound anything like the real thing that came to sing at the end of the garden every May, its dependable call comforted me through many a sleepless night.

This Dutch clock was the inspiration for the first song I ever learned. One evening as I wound its metal key, my father taught me a song that was very popular at the time – 'My Grandfather's Clock', about the relationship between an old man and his faithful time-keeper. I cannot have been more than five years old, and I was enthralled and intrigued by the tune and the words, composed by a Chicago printer, Henry Clay Work, in 1876. I read much later that his songs, and surely this one, were inspired by the noises of the printing machines that surrounded him.

> *Ninety years without slumbering; tick-tock, tick-tock.*
> *Its life-seconds numbering; tick-tock, tick-tock.*
> *It stopped short, never to go again.*
> *When the old man died.*

It struck an alarm in the middle of the night;
An alarm that for years had been dumb.
And we knew that his spirit was pluming for flight.
That his hour of departure had come.
Yet the clock went its round with a low and muf-
fled sound.
As we silently stood by its side.
And it stopped short never to go again.
When the old man died.

I had never heard the term 'pluming for flight' before, and I was convinced that, instead of dying, the old man was preparing to pack his travel bags for a long journey. In a way, I suppose he was. Death is the ultimate solo flight to the eternal. Oddly, it has remained a theme song all through my life, and sometimes I sing my own version of it. Indeed it has been commented on many times, including a mention by the *Irish Times* critic Charles Acton following a concert I shared with the late, great tenor, Frank Patterson. 'Then Nóirín Ní Riain sang for a quarter of an hour … and it was fascinating to hear her adding *sean-nós* ornaments to the song "Grandfather's Clock".'

What's in a Name?

LL NAMES TO ME ARE CREATIVE AND mesmerising. I believe that in Western society, we have lost respect and reverence for the power that the hallowed sound of our names hold. From a very young age I was spellbound by the sound of the divine names of God, Mary and Jesus. I knew that I could call on God and that, far from being a distant deity, this Holy One was someone whom I could call on *by name*.

God's name is the common denominator in the Bible. Scripture recalls how the sound of the name of God dispels the darkness of the night. From out of this sound, the morning darkness dims to lay bare the hallowed name. 'For lo, the one who forms the mountains, creates the wind, reveals his thoughts to mortals, makes the morning darkness, and treads on the heights of the earth – the Lord, the God of hosts, is his name!' (Amos 4:13). It was no surprise to learn later that Jesus Christ named and called this same God by the pet name of Abba/Father and urged every Christian to prayer to 'Our Father' (Matthew 6:9). Every Christian is privileged to nominate God 'Father'.

The psalmist foretells the great Christ event: 'O Lord … how majestic is your name in all the earth!' (Psalm 8:1) Through Jesus Christ, the echo of God's name is sounded once and for all. 'The naming of God ... is not simple ... It is not a single tone, but polyphonic,' philosopher Paul Ricouer suggests, using sonic imagery.[1]

The name for God in the Irish language is '*Dia*'. Prayer as dialogue becomes *Dia-logue* – a nearest and dearest conversation between God's logos and the praying one who is known by and in the image of that divine word.

The name 'Jesus' represents the Hebrew and Aramaic *yesu'a*, which is a late form of the Hebrew *yehosu'a*. It is a 'theophoric' name, which means that it embraces some divine name or title of God in its make-up. To be given the name of Jesus is to be called 'Yahweh is salvation'. Jesus is true to his name; he is the saviour who carries the authority of God. Jesus lived by his saving name. His followers and disciples followed suit: the name of Jesus carried status. Angelus Silesius, the German mystic who converted to Roman Catholicism in 1653, was convinced of the power of this Jesus name: 'The name of Jesus is an oil poured out and spilt, It nourishes and shines, the soul's own woe it stills.'[2] And to address the Divine human one in Irish is beautiful: '*A Íosa!*'

—

I was baptised Nora Mary Antoinette Ryan. 'Nora' came from my mother, and indeed her mother before her. I am Nora the Third. 'Antoinette' has to do with the date on which I was born. My mother prayed that I would appear on the feast of St Anthony, 13 June. But, disappointingly for her, I appeared on the twelfth! 'Disobedient in birth as in life', she occasionally reminded me!

1. Paul Ricoeur, *Figuring the Sacred*, Augsburg Fortress Publishers, 1995, p. 224.

2. Angelus Silesius, *The Cherubinic Wanderer*, translated by Maria Shrady, Paulist Press, 1986, p. 87.

21

One evening, as we sat by the Aga cooker, I asked her where the 'Mary' in my name came from. She replied, 'Ah, no rhyme or reason. Sure, everyone was called Mary, even men'. Through the simple question, I had plucked a fragile chord. She went on to tell me about one particular Irishman called Joseph Mary Plunkett, a Dubliner executed in the 1916 Rising at the age of thirty-one. She was two years old, she added. I still remember the sound of her voice as she wistfully recited his lovely religious poem, 'The Presence of God'. The symbol of the Divine in the thunder and the singing of God's voice stood out loud and clear as she spoke.

> I see his blood upon the rose
> And in the stars the glory of his eyes,
> His body gleams amid eternal snows,
> His tears fall from the skies.
>
> I see his face in every flower,
> The thunder and the singing of the birds
> Are but his voice – and carven by his power
> Rocks are his written words.
>
> All pathways by his feet are worn,
> His strong heart sits the ever-beating sea,
> His crown of thorns is twined with every thorn,
> His cross is every tree.

'Mary' comes from the Greek names 'Maria' or 'Mariam' and the Hebrew 'Miryam'. Mary is not just a name but is also a title referring to a singing role which women played in antiquity. The Exodus drama of salvation when performed by early ascetics had two choirs: one of men directed by a singer representing Moses; the other of women led by a woman singer, Miriam. Mary of Magdala and Mary of Nazareth could well have been singers in their own lives untold of in the gospels, using their voices to pray to God. So naming me Mary was perhaps no accident at all!

One Life with God and Song

MY PARENTS SAID THAT I SANG long before I spoke. Childhood was lonesome and solitary – I was a troubled child. When a stranger would approach my little wooden playpen, I would run to the other side, burying my tearful eyes under my right elbow, literally keeping everyone at arm's length. Even then I had some inner fear and distrust that would plague me all my life, revealing itself in a crippling anxiety before singing for people.

Very early on, I created my own imaginary world where I was sheltered and at home with an invisible special friend – God, who in turn affectionately called me Noreen Mary Antoinette. There was no uncertainty, shyness or anxiety in my relationship with the Absolute. In this other space, singing for God was my own experience of what the Roman poet Horace observed two thousand years ago: '*Minuentur atrae, Carmine curae*' – Dark worries will be lessened by song.

Somehow, I was destined to live in this solitary terrain. God was my secret, very best soulmate, to whom I talked, sang and listened, day in, day out. Neither my parents nor anybody else realised that, very early on, I created a relationship with some spiritual presence that was going to accompany me, be my right hand 'person' through life. It is interesting that the word 'person' comes from two Latin words: *'per'* meaning 'through' and 'son' from *'sonare'*, meaning 'sound'. Looking back on it now, I clearly see that the basis of my relationship with God has been through sound and the ear.

I always knew that I had a guardian angel, and many other angel friends besides. They were always listening to me and I prayed to them all, night and day. 'Oh Angel of God, my guardian dear, to whom God's love commits me *hear* … ' Years later when I saw the written version, I realised that the word was, rather, 'here'!

Some twenty years ago, I stumbled on America's most famous spiritual poet, Emily Dickinson. Her precise poetic expression of belief in and relationship with angels is music to my ears, capturing my youthful angelic experience too.

> God permits industrious Angels –
> Afternoons – to play –
> I met one – forgot my Schoolmates –
> All – for Him – straightway –
> God calls home – the Angels – promptly –
> At the Setting Sun –
> I missed him – how dreary – Marbles –
> After playing Crown![3]

3. *The Complete Poems of Emily Dickinson*, edited by Thomas H. Johnson, Faber and Faber, 1970, p. 105.

Mother–Teacher, Father–Holy Man

MY MOTHER WAS A PRIMARY school teacher working in a school five miles from home, in the next parish. A great educator, she respected her students. 'Those who have taught many to do what is right shall be like the stars forever and ever' (Daniel 12:3). We travelled together to that faraway parish of Caherline every day. My school pals lived miles away and so were never my home pals. And indeed, being teacher's daughter in teacher's class was an isolating experience. From the ages of six to nine, I sat in her classroom knowing her as *my mother*. I was so proud of her, of all the poetry and knowledge that she embodied, of her voice, her beauty. Yet she could not, of course, show any affection to me or appreciation of any signs of my achievements. But it can't have been easy for her, and, all in all, she adopted a balanced approach to it.

One school memory stands out. I remember sitting in the two-seater bench. My mother's older sister, a St Louis nun, Sr Rumold, had given me a book of Irish legends, which I had never opened. Ma brought this to school and introduced us to a great Celtic mythological tale that excited all our interests there and then. First she had us chant: '*Tá cluasa capaill ag an Rí, Tá cluasa capaill ag an Rí ...*' (The king has horse's ears) on one note, a monotone, the first accent being on the 'clu' of the '*cluasa*'. Then my mother acted the entire mythical drama out, with the same vocal nuances of her one-to-one reciting of Plunkett's 'Presence of God'.

> *Fadó, fadó,* there lived a mighty king called Labhrás Ó Loinsigh. Greatly loved by all his people, he was plagued by a skeleton in the cupboard: he was born with horse's ears. Nobody was to know of this endowment. To become a king, one must be physically whole with no element of imperfection. So he let his beautiful locks hush-hush the secret. Once a year, he had his hair cut by a young barber, who would then vanish, never to be seen again, because they alone shared the secret. This year however, the young man doing the haircutting job overheard the King's neurotic plan to have him disappear, and went to him pleading, '*Éist liom* (Listen to me), O Royal King. Let me go free. I am the only child of a widow and I promise you, on my very word, that I will not tell any living soul about what I have seen'.
>
> The King obediently listened and granted the youth his freedom. But the undisclosed information was too heavy a load for the young haircutter to carry. So he went to 'confession' to a respected druid who advised him to go deep into the forest and whisper his royal discovery to a large oak tree. Convinced that his 'penance'

was secure, since this mighty tree was no living soul, and feeling that his profession was safe, he returned home light of heart.

In the meantime, King Labhrás commissioned a brand new harp which would be heard in all of his great assemblies. Three of the finest wood-cutters were ordered to select and cut down the noblest of the forest oak trees; three of the most reputable harp makers were then to go to work, and in three weeks the most superb harp was presented to the king at a banquet of superlative quality with all the elite. After a magnificent dinner, the court harper sat before the harp but the oak musical piece would only chant: '*Tá cluasa capaill ag an Rí*' ...

Speaking this fable, Ma sculpted my sense of hearing. I often longed to know the sequel. What happened when word was out? Surely he lost none of his loving subjects nor any of his true followers?

Mother had some sense of the power, the magic of the aural. There was a beautiful large seashell which she treasured and kept on the front step of Mount Marian. 'Take it up and listen to it,' she would say, 'and you'll hear the sound of the sea.' Many's the time I repeated the ritual and many's the time I heard that vast noisy ocean. The object is the shell but the inherited sound of that roaring sea, the song which that seashell has imbibed from the ocean, still continues to resound, to hold the drone faithfully, long after the shell has been tugged from its natural home and family.

Paddy Ryan was a holy man. A daily Massgoer, he talked about going to 'hear Mass' before he went to

work. 'As long as I can tie my shoelaces, I'll go to hear
Mass,' he declared. But I could never really understand this phrase then because I watched him every
Sunday at Mass not listening at all! To 'hear Mass' for
him meant to barely whisper an entire round of the
Rosary. He always carried a Rosary beads in some
pocket. I inherited this formalistic spirituality from
him of 'hearing daily Mass', and I also say the Rosary
most days (although never during Mass), and the
beads are always on me. Travelling in the car with him,
he constantly reminded me to bless myself at the sight
of every church, and I still do. Mind you, back then I
was often confused as to why some churches didn't
seem to warrant this particular salutation!

Without realising it, I picked up a lot about language and listening from both parents. My mother was
very creative with words. 'That's doldiedi altogether'
was her response when she just did not agree with you.
An even stronger put-down was 'Oh, tupenny doll-
talk'! And some of my physical responses are still
grounded in sounds of my childhood. A yawn is always
'uh, huh, hodio', inherited from my loving father as he
yawned his way through cooking his early morning
breakfast of bacon and eggs. Even then, I sensed that
there is something hidden and mysterious in every
sound that must be listened out for to be experienced.
'Let me hear of your steadfast love in the morning'
(Psalm 143:8).

Silence is not always Golden

MY MOUNT MARIAN YOUTH WAS made up of many long, lonely silences, which I loathed. Marion, my sister, and Noel, my brother, had left for boarding school by the time I was nine and I sometimes felt like an only child alone there in the house. Although I loved my mother dearly and knew that she loved me, sometimes I could not bear her silences and only craved her attention and praise.

One Sunday morning stands out in my memory. My parents and I had a ritual: after 11 o'clock Mass in Caherline, we'd stop at the shop to buy the paper. Once we reached the stained-glass front door of home, Mother and I would go up the stairs to change out of our Sunday best before preparing lunch together. I loved this time because I had her all to myself – even our maid, as family helpers were called then, had the day off. My role of peeling the potatoes and setting the table always excited my young heart. I was the indispensable little lady.

While all of this was going on, Da would sit out in his car reading that Sunday paper. Sometimes I'd ask him why he wouldn't come inside and join us; there were plenty of solitary spaces in our home. 'Well, it's quiet

here I suppose. So go on now and I'll be in shortly.'
Looking back, I think he valued that air of silence particularly in his fancy dark green Volvo. So, paper read,
Da would appear just as Mother and I were ready to
serve and share Sunday lunch. My father loved to hear
me sing at any time. So one Sunday he ordered, 'Give
us a tune, pet'. He sat down at the table and I burst
forth with a Burt Bacharach hit that was all the rage
then and that I had heard on Radio Luxembourg.
'*If I were a tower of strength, I'd walk away, I'd look
in your eyes and here's what I'd say …* ' I belted it out,
adding all the appropriate gyrations. My father smiled
in amusement, but Ma simply glared at me in disgust
and disappeared out the kitchen door without a word.

Father and daughter became eating companions
that afternoon. He told me that he disapproved of
Mother's behaviour, but that did little to alleviate my
pain at having shocked and disappointed her with a
bawdy pop song. He took to the bed for his usual Sunday siesta and I spent the rest of the afternoon alone.
By dusk there was still no sign of her, so I went into the
back of the garage where she kept the grain to feed the
hens. And there she was, in the driver seat of her green
Morris Minor car, in another realm of green-car
silence. 'Ma,' I stammered, 'I'm sorry. I won't ever sing
that song again. Da and I, we kept a bit of dinner in the
oven for you.' 'Thanks,' she replied and, glad of the
excuse perhaps, went back into the house. Like with
the hens, I didn't want her going hungry.

> Words move, music moves
> Only in time; but that which is only living
> Can only die. Words, after speech, reach

4. T.S. Eliot, 'Burnt Norton', *The Complete Poems and Plays of T.S. Eliot*, Faber and Faber, 1969, p. 175.

Into the silence. Only by the form, the pattern,
Can words or music reach
The stillness, as a Chinese jar still
Moves perpetually in its stillness.[4]

First Strains of Plainchant

IN THE LATE 1950S AND THE 1960S, BEFORE the full impact of Vatican II's decrees on plainchant was known, Latin was the language and plainchant was the sound of the Mass. Most Sundays for six years, I sat up beside my mother, the director of the parish school choir, as her 'first cantor' in the little wooden choir pen at the back of the 'old' Caherline church. In her young days, actually well into her seventies until a life of heavy smoking took its toll, she was a fine, natural singer. I owe my introduction to plainchant completely to her.

The timelessness of the silver sound of plainchant springs from her singing us in with, 'Now after three: one, two three', which bore no relationship whatsoever to the rhythm. Out of an extended pause, we somehow managed to start together. This really was 'in God's own time'! We sang chants such as the Kyrie and Gloria from the suitably named 'Missa de Angelis', the Mass of the Angels.

Plainchant is pure prayer for singer and listener alike. The Scottish writer and historian, Thomas Carlyle, once described song as 'little dew-drops of celestial melody'. This is the most apt description for me of plainchant, the ancient aural icon of the entire Christian story. Although preferred to the term 'Gregorian chant' since the thirteenth century, plainchant has nothing ordinary, dull or unattractive about it; the English term simply derives from two Latin words: '*cantus*' and '*planus*', which together mean unmeasured or non-rhythmic song. Preserved in manuscripts from the ninth century and still the heart of the monastic daily prayer stops, the prayerful possibility and life-giving power of each chant resides in the very sound itself, confirming the command of the great Judaeo-Christian prophet, Isaiah: 'Listen that you may live.'

Plainchant is beautiful, consoling, disturbing, sometimes surprising but always moving. It is thanksgiving. Certain chants are bright and luminous; others are calm, soft and hushed. Syllabic chants are those that go with the flow of the Latin words, syllable by syllable. Melismatic chants, on the other hand, are adorned with a seemingly endless number of notes that heighten the words. Sometimes plainchant faintly echoes the very old humming world between the Hebrew Scriptures and the New Testament; sometimes it reverberates with melodic resonances of new life in the coming Kingdom of God.

As *sean-nós* – traditional Irish folk singing – is to the soul of Ireland, so plainsong is to the heart of Christianity. Singing and listening to this oldest song of the Christ story can shape each day with new growth and healing, and it still remains at the core of monastic liturgies. '*Bis orat qui cantat*' is an ancient proverb with a timeless, universal truth: 'The one who sings prays twice.' '*Bis orat qui audit*' is the descant, an independent melody which perfectly harmonises with this saying: 'The one who *listens* (with the ear of the heart) prays twice.'

34

Two 'Aunty Nuns'

Come pensive Nun, devout and pure,
Sober, steadfast and demure,
All in a robe of darkest grain
Flowing with majestic train ...
                    – 'Il Penseroso', John Milton

TWO OF MY MOTHER'S SISTERS – THE 'aunty nuns' we called them – entered the religious life and were, like herself, 'national' school teachers. The younger, Agg, was a Presentation sister, and chose the name 'Paschal' for her religious life; the older was a St Louis sister, Sr Rumold, who later returned to her family name of Mary Hassett. We knew her as Auntie Mai.

Words were a Hassett sister obsession. Their days of old age unfolded through the proud completion of the *Irish Times* crossword. Although unaware of it, I treasured the evenings when these three teachers sat around the kitchen table and talked. There was a fertility, a spirit about their quaint conversations. I think it was the sound of their voices too that enthralled me. All three were lovely singers, and over the years the two aunts taught me many songs during these holiday visits.

I was particularly close to Auntie Mai, especially towards the end of her long life of ninety-four years. A great reader, she provided me with a wide-ranging spiritual library which sculpted my life. For my first communion it was *Children's Stories from the Bible*. I read and re-read these stories aloud about my own friend, God. The reading was always aloud because, for me, the silent stories had to be spoken to be understood, had to be heard to be believed. I loved the picture on the cover of this book. On the right was the romantic figure of a handsome, long-haired, bearded man – my own image of God – knocking on a large wooden door and listening intently to what was happening on the other side. On the left side of the cover was a gathering of multicultural children waiting intently, ear-first, for God to enter. I often imagined that I was in the midst of these children, on the other side of the door, listening and hearing, and the odd time singing my troubled heart out to them all.

Through constant practice, I became very good at hearing and listening to this *anam chara*, this soul friend. This is what being lonesome and apart does, and continues to do. It gives you keys that open the doors to the Divine. Nineteenth-century English art critic and author, John Ruskin, spent his entire childhood playing with only a bunch of old keys! The sound of the keys, lightly touched and in time, were his existence. 'All one's life is music, if one touches the notes rightly and in time,' he said. For me, the newfound key that unlocked my resourcefulness was that Bible-cover image of the ever-listening God.

The Little Priestess

I CAN'T REMEMBER EXACTLY WHEN I FIRST began the ritual of stealing into my parents' bedroom to 'say' Mass. But I can recall vividly the moment when the whole fantasy fell apart. Every day, around 4 o'clock, that parental bedroom became a private chapel where I 'said', rather than 'heard', Mass. The centrepiece of that room was a small fireplace of brown and grey tiles, which faced the big bay window. I would stand up on the little ledge of the fireplace and, being ahead of my time, face out towards the congregation. The gangly oak tree outside danced and sang. 'For you shall go out in joy, and be led back in peace … and all the trees of the field shall clap their hands' (Isaiah 55:12).

To the left of the 'altar', the ledge of the fireplace, was a statue of Mary. At its dead centre was a black and white crucifix with a three-dimensional image of Jesus. With Mother and Father safely away, I imagined the room was full of characters all hanging on my every word for redemption and salvation. We quietly chanted the 'Our Father' together, and I sang 'Regina Caeli' and 'Adoro Te Devote' while my invisible flock made their way towards me for Holy Communion, which I doled out to them in the form of round white mints.

My 'sacristy' was the landing outside the door. Now one afternoon, I passed my big brother there after I had just said Mass. 'Noel, I'm going to be a priest when I grow up,' I told him excitedly. 'Don't be so ridiculous, Noreen. You can't even be an altar boy, not to talk of a priest!' That was the first time I realised that the priest saying Mass every Sunday at Caherline would never be a woman. Devastated that I might never minister to humans, my mission then became to convert – at the very least – the animals around me! Very little conversion was needed; animals have an innate sense of the spiritual and the silence.

I started with my little cocker spaniel, Banner. After school each day, when all the poor dog wanted was to be taken for a walk, I would first insist that we bless the walk with a prayer. As I'd tickle him under his front paws and sing to him, he'd wriggle his little head from side to side with pleasure. I firmly believed that he was really sent to me from his anagrammatic namesake, God.

I then progressed onto my mother's hens. They supplied us with what are now called 'organic' eggs and, to show my thanks, I vowed to bring them to God through listening. Every morning and evening, with my little *sugán* chair under my arm, I invaded the hen house and insisted that these foul fowl sing the 'Our Father' to be saved. And as I chanted each line, I waited for them to respond. And they did, they did. Henpecked into conversion.

Glenstal Abbey – Heart-Home

As a young girl, I was drawn to an alternative home-space just a few miles from our house – Glenstal Abbey, the only male Benedictine monastery in Ireland. Little did I realise back then that the sacred space and its residents were to become friends for life. Glenstal Abbey has been a relentlessly safe harbour and my spiritual home for over fifty years now.

At that time, the locals had the impression that these monks on the hill in Murroe were rather snobby and standoffish. I remember a family friend saying: 'Oh, *Glenstaawl* – you'd have to polish your shoes before you walked up that avenue.' However, when the new public chapel was opened and blessed on Sunday 24 June 1956, there was great excitement in the locality. My mother bundled me into her Morris Minor and off we went to witness the event.

Although I was only very young when this public chapel opened, I can still faintly recall the extraordinary song and sound of the monks that afternoon. The fact that it was an all-male community was lost on me – I had yet to learn from Noel's insight! The beguiling sound of chant touched a chord way beyond anything I had ever known before. That was my first glimpse of an unknown otherness that could be accessed through singing. It was my very first step on a pathway towards something mysterious and wondrous. From that day on, I was to walk many times through that 'darkest valley, where I fear no evil; for you are with me ...' (Psalm 23:4).

After that, I would regularly cycle the six miles from our home to Glenstal. I was, and still am, much firmer on my feet than on wheels, so I'd dump the bike at the gates and walk up the avenue lined with its oak tree residents, which were, still are, will always be the imposing guardians of the estate. They are emblems of strength and hospitality. Their massive trunks and limbs cared for and sheltered me. Sometimes in the pouring rain, I would stand in under one of them; the numbed pitter-patter of the rain falling gently on the leaves above me was music to my ears and comfort for my soul. I really believed that God sang these trees into creation, and that they were in turn, as the psalm sings it, shouting for joy at the presence of the Lord. I would day-dream that I was one of those sprawling oak trees. To thrive, just like them, I needed nourishment, sunshine and rain (which the Native Americans call 'liquid sunshine'). My young body suddenly resonated with these trees in sound and stillness – I had stumbled on a sacred space between heaven and earth.

The oak is a sacred tree. Jewish Scripture is teeming with oak-tree events. Deborah, Rebekah's nurse, was buried under an oak (Genesis 35:8). Jacob buried all foreign gods and earrings under the Shechem oak (Genesis 35:4). There is the oak in the sanctuary of the Lord where Joshua placed his holy book in the last chapter of the first book of his own name (24:26). The man of God from Judah in the first book of Kings is found sitting in the shade of the oak (13:14). Saul and his sons are buried under the Jabesh oak (1 Chronicles 10:12). But my favourite oak tale of all is in the Book of Judges. In Ophrah, Gideon is in the wine press when God's angel comes and sits under his father's oak tree. 'The Lord is with you ... do not fear ... I will be with you' (Judges 6:11-24). This story beautifully paves the pathway for me to the great aural promise of God's angel Gabriel to Mary when she conceived through the sound of Gabriel's golden voice. 'The angel said to her, "Do not be afraid, Mary, for you have found favour with God"' (Luke 1:30).

Celtic tradition is also rich with tales of and references to the enchanting, bewitching oak. The ancient story of the oak tree harp that could not keep the secret of Labhrás Ó Loinsigh has already been told here. In Irish this tree is called '*dair*', which is the source of the word 'druid', a title for a wise person, an elder, or a priest. It is no coincidence then that the front avenue of Glenstal Abbey is overflowing with *dair*. Truly this was a space set apart for ritual and liturgy long, long before these contemporary monastic druids made it their home.

A little anecdote about the legendary oak. The one-acre garden in Mount Marian was carefully maintained by an old local gardener, Jim. A very spiritual man, he had tremendous respect and reverence for each little plant he handled and gently placed in the soil. One spring morning when I was about ten, he was planting a small oak tree and I was playing with Banner. As he stood back observing the sturdy little tree in its new home in the ground, he was moved to share a rather bizarre memory. 'Years ago, girleen, I once felled an

41

oak tree, and honest to God, as it fell to the ground, it let out an almighty roar like an old man. If you gave me a thousand pounds, I'd never cut one down again. I never want to hear that scream again as long as I live.' From that day on, I always cautiously eyed this little woody perennial plant.

Quite apart from the oaks, I have constantly been drawn to the Abbey's monastic graveyard. Something about that world, inhabited by those who have passed over, awakened in me a love of burial grounds. The silence of that cemetery has no black rhythms about it, no fragments of fear. To this day, wherever I find myself in my travels, wandering through 'God's acre', the dead centre of the place, is always part of the itinerary. The early draw to the Glenstal graveyard for me was around the tragic biography of the original owners, the Barringtons, who built the romantic Norman castle in 1839. The story was very familiar to all in the locality. The young daughter of the house, Winefred, was 'going out' with an English officer. One May afternoon in 1921, when the two were out driving, she had on her the soldier's army cap. Mistaking Winnie for her lover, some Republicans shot and killed the only daughter of the house and she died later that evening. (Shortly after, the family abandoned the estate, and in 1925 they offered it to the Irish Free State government as a presidential residence. But Dublin was too far away for this to be practical, so in 1926 it fell into the hands of a priest, Monsignor James Ryan, who thought to establish a Benedictine community. He had a long-standing friendship with an Irish Benedictine abbot in Maredsous in Belgium, who sent five of his Belgian monks to Glenstal Abbey on 18 April 1927.) Winnie's voice still

echoes through the stone walls, particularly on wet,
grey days in the 'Lady Garden', adjacent to the monastic cemetery. Fifty years later, I am walking, breathing
and talking easily to God in all these sacred places of
Glenstal Abbey.

Somewhere Over the Rainbow

THE YEAR 1958, TWO YEARS AFTER MY first conscious memories of plainchant, was an important one in my singing life. In May of that year my father, Paddy, turned fifty and held a big party, not so rare an event in Mount Marian. Family and friends crowded into our house and it filled with song. Both my parents were natural, untrained singers; Nora's party piece was 'Scarlet Ribbons', while Paddy's was, 'I'll Take You Home Again, Kathleen'. These two songs still have a life of their own for me and I hear them regularly in day and night dreams.

I managed to stay up late by slipping in and out of every room, timing it just long enough not to be adult-spotted. Eventually, I was discovered and sent straight up to bed. But I soon tiptoed out again, and dressed in my pink, flowery cotton nightdress, sat on the top step of the stairs for a long time, listening intently to the adults singing below. Among the familiar voices of uncles and aunts was a female voice I could not recognise. Her singing brightened every corner of the house. Hours later, when the party wound down and the revellers went home, I crept into bed. Da, glowing from high spirits in every sense of the word, tottered into my

bedroom. His towering silhouette announced, 'We're
going to take you into Limerick for singing lessons.
There was a singer here tonight and she said that she'll
teach you'.

My vocal and life teacher for the next five years was
to be this invisible voice of that May evening. On
Wednesdays at 4.30 p.m., my mother would drive me
into Roches Street in Limerick where Mary McDon-
agh taught me singing and a whole lot more. In the living room above her mother's grocery shop, Mary set
me on the road to becoming a public singer. She
quickly became my idol.

The first song she taught me was 'Somewhere Over
the Rainbow' from *The Wizard of Oz*. Like me, the
heroine Dorothy was an introverted little girl who
sought personal happiness in her song. *'Someday, I'll
wish upon a star and wake up where the clouds are far
behind me. Where troubles melt like lemon drops away
above the chimney tops, that's where you'll find me.'*

My father's smaller sister, in age if not size, was
Auntie B, and she was my first fan. Everyone loved
Biddy, this enormous, earthy woman. She married into
a bar and grocery shop in Caherconlish and she would
lean her heavy breasts over the counter when we called
in for messages, always curious about how we were
getting on. When my teacher, Mary, entered me for
competitions, Auntie B sat up in the front row. Thanks
to Mary, who was a true professional and taught me all
the tricks of the trade, I was streets ahead of my peers
when it came to performance skills. I carried away first
prizes in Féile Luimní, even when I competed against
older age-groups. Auntie Biddy, high-spirited after the
adjudication, would insist on treating myself and Ma

to an enormous afternoon tea in Limerick's Stella Café after each win. She was marvellously generous, always slipping me a half crown when she got out of the car, and always encouraging.

Dún Lughaidh Exile

THIS CHILDHOOD, DEVOTED TO GOD and singing, changed for ever when I entered boarding school at the age of eleven. Here I was alienated from the ear of the heart. My sister, Marion, had been sent to a convent boarding school nearby when she was twelve and I was just five. So I already had a sense of this privileged secondary education. Although we were not very close as sisters at that time, I looked forward to the frequent visits we made to this exotic female. When it came time for me to go to second-level, my parents decided to send me further afield, to St Louis Convent, Dundalk, where Ma's older sister, Auntie Mai, resided and taught.

My mother spent her summer holidays of 1962 carefully sewing name tags onto my entire secondary school uniform and painstakingly packing two enormous grey suitcases. I had to bid farewell to my dearest little canine disciple, cocker spaniel Banner. For weeks beforehand he could sense that I was leaving, and for as many nights spent them sleeping in the half-packed cases on my bedroom floor, begging me in his own doggy way not to go. (Two months later Banner got distemper and died, and I still regret not being with him to bless his final moments.)

Finally, one morning in late August, we loaded the two large grey cases into the boot of the green Volvo. On top was a cardboard box containing my favourite fruit cake, wrapped in grease-proof paper, which Mother had baked the day before, and two packets of my much-loved biscuits, Kimberly and Marietta. How would I be ever hungry again!

Auntie B joined us on the three-hundred-mile journey to my new abode. She carefully placed a brightly coloured parcel on top of my tuck box before sitting into the back seat beside me and slapping my lap. 'Now you'll have to keep singing for us all the way to Dundalk,' she said. And I think I actually did, having no idea, thank God, of the ordeal my voice and being were about to undergo and the loneliness that the next six years would hold.

On our arrival at this new place of discovery, as we drove through the gate, I first noticed the castle to the left and a vision of Glenstal Abbey fleetingly came and went. Auntie Mai was waiting for us at the front door of that large, grey school building, and we unloaded the car. My ears were deafened by the hustle and bustle along the resonant corridors of two hundred young girls settling in. 'All juniors sleep in the castle,' Auntie Mai said, as we climbed the narrow stairs to the bare dormitory of ten little beds. I was frightened and already feeling lonesome, and crouched beside my assigned cubicle while Ma and her sister made up my bed.

Then Auntie B produced her wrapped box. Inside was a very expensive pink, sequinned jewellery box, and when I opened the lid, a tiny embracing couple sprang up and pirouetted to the tune of 'The Anniversary Waltz'. That was Auntie B alright, full of impractical

generosity! An anniversary jewellery gift box was the
last present that an eleven-year-old about to embark
on a solitary boarding school experience would need.
And yet I grew to love that little music box. To listen to
its song, to see the happy couple dance in harmony, it
had to be wound up with a metal key. This ritual
brought some comfort, resonating with winding memories of the Mount Marian cuckoo clock. There were
many, many times when I wound the key, lifted the lid
and just listened, comforted by an echo of home in
some way.

Two fragile yet intuitive thoughts just about helped
this little eleven-year-old gather her broken heart
together and bravely wave goodbye to her family trio as
they drove out of sight through the large wrought-iron
gates. I knew for the first time that I would now have to
make it through on my own. And there was something,
someone else at work here – a Divine source, a friendly
voice who promised to guide and bless me through it all.

Everything about Dún Lughaidh was alien to me, even
the landscape. I was at home in Limerick's level and
smooth horizon, yet here I was trapped in a stark stone
building on the outskirts of Dundalk with the
unfriendly Mourne Mountains towering over. Before I
knew the correct spelling, I often thought that their
name was appropriate: the Mourns. The wind from
this great mountain range was bitter and biting and
seemed to constantly blow around us during our com-
pulsory afternoon walks. Before I had ever adopted the
beautiful Psalm 121 as my constant daily anthem,
I remember silently calling to these sad, far-off hills – 'I
lift up my eyes to the hills – from where will my help

come? My help comes from the Lord, who made heaven and earth.'

I needed all the help I could get because I felt like more of an outsider now than ever before. My school-mates ridiculed my southern accent, mimicking my greeting of 'how are you'. And I had problems under-standing their own northern drawls. The nuns and teachers were constantly correcting me and insisting that I lower my 'boisterous, vulgar voice' in the echoey corridors and in the dormitories, although I was unaware of being so loud. Sr Giovanni, a fine headmistress at the time, was a staunch Gaelgóir and insisted on addressing us in Irish. But her accent, indeed the entire school's dialect, was rooted in the Gaoth Dobhair, Donegal pronunciation. Mine was a Southern, Cork/Kerry pro-nunciation and I was lost, unable to communicate.

Meal times were the biggest shock to the system. On a lucky day, the main dish was practically scraped bare as it passed from the seniors to us juniors at the bottom of the table. On an unlucky day, when the food was less tasty, there was plenty left and I'd have to eat some of it. The contents of my tuck box disappeared faster than I could ever have imagined, and I was often so hungry that I coated my tongue with nail varnish to make up for lack of food. God alone knows why this hunger preventative didn't make me ill.

I was set apart from the very first morning, when the entire school assembled in the concert hall. Suddenly the door swung open and in marched Sr Giovanni. We stood to say a prayer for the New Year and welcomes were extended to all who were returning.

'But a special welcome to the girls who are joining us for the first time.' Then the surprise! 'We particularly

welcome Sr Rumold's niece. We hear that she is a
beautiful singer.' The headmistress sounded a little
caustic as she continued: 'Maybe she will sing us a song
now?' This did serious damage to my image and it
marked me apart from the beginning. Being singled
out at any age requires very great humility and grace,
which I certainly did not have! 'Precocious' was the
word for me then, having been taught and developing
singing abilities beyond my years. So up I confidently
leapt, and launched into my first party piece. These
lyrics were to be prophetic as I spent most of the next
years wishing to be somewhere else: *'If happy little blue-birds fly beyond the rainbow, why, oh why, can't I?'*

Being Sr Rumold's niece put me at a distinct disad-vantage with pupils and teachers alike. To my peers
I was 'Blue Mould's pet'. They'd spy her coming into
the dorm, tidying my bed or leaving a bar of chocolate
under my pillow. That was the impetus for them to play
some new trick on me. Like pulling back the blankets
and scattering bath salts between the sheets. Bed
clothes carefully restored, they'd wait for my shocked
reaction at lights-out and smother their tittering as I'd
tearfully sweep away the prickly crystals.

As for the teachers, the fact that Sr Rumold was my
aunt meant that I was under special scrutiny. Any time
I strayed off the straight and narrow, academically or
behaviourally, she was the first person to be told. This
happened frequently, and before long I could detect
from the sound of her step on the long corridors the
measure of the trouble I was in!

Although I had experienced lonely times at home in
Mount Marian, the yearning of my teenage years took
on a whole different resonance. Remaining in the silent

'hear and now' provided an enormous treasure-trove of riches for living and praying. My inner friend and I alone again, we spoke the same language, shared the same silence perfectly. During these formative years, I discovered that our hearing ears are the locus and source of all human interconnectedness, including our relationship with God. To put it another way, the membrane of your inner ear, which allows such precise and constant access to all that is beyond us, is one of the most privileged inlets to God. To ignore this aural relationship, to turn deaf ears to the ear of the heart is to remain constantly on the defensive.

Throughout the Louis years, there was one early morning sound that I longed for. It was the Mount Marian cock crow among Mother's hens. But in the senior years there, I made do with opening up the frosted dorm window of my cubicle from where I could see a little silent weather cock on a faraway church spire.

I was fascinated by these weather vanes, as they are sometimes called and which still adorn some churches. The cock has the four directions of North, South, East and West indicated on its comb. 'Chanticleer' is an ancient medieval name for a rooster, a fusion of two French words, '*chanter*' and '*claire*' – the 'clear singer'. The cock is an audiocentric symbol with its own folk-loric tale around its voice/sound (one and the same meaning in Hebrew, Greek and Irish too). Sometime during those latter years in Dún Lughaidh, our English teacher, Sr De La Salle, taught us a poem by Francis Ledwidge entitled 'Chanticleer'. I silently wondered at the last line of each verse, what it meant and why the poet might have tagged on the Irish five-syllable line, '*Mac na hÓighe Slán*' (The Son of Mary is saved).

Much later, I heard an Irish spin on the biblical Golgotha Hill tale of death and resurrection, which the poet must surely have heard also. It not only satisfied my curiousity but educated me in yet another way to tune into the ear of the heart; all sounds, even farm animal song, can carry the sound of God.

> After Christ's death on the cross, Pontius Pilate returned home for his supper, for which his wife was boiling a rooster. Pontius sat down ponderously at the table and said, 'I have done a terrible deed this day. I have just killed the Son of God.' 'Don't be ridiculous,' said his wife. 'It's as likely that you killed God's Son today as it is that this rooster will fly up out of this pot.' At that moment, the cock rose up and sang, '*Mac na hÓighe Slán*'.

Although we learned the entire poem off by heart, I can only recite a fragment of it now:

> A gaudy bird that stalks in pride
> About the farmyard all day long.
> A legend tells at Christmastide
> It heard the angels' song:
> And it flew to Mary's side
> When first the mystic starlight shone.
> And sent the message far and wide,
> *Mac na hÓighe Slán*.
>
> And still when in the lonely tomb
> The mangled form of Jesus lay.
> And all the world was wrapped in glow,
> It watched by night and day;

53

And when the Easter morning broke,
And danced the sun upon the dawn
To the risen Christ again is spoke,
Mac na hÓighe Slán.

Legend has it that the sixth-century Irish saint, Colmán, had a chanticleer, a bright shining voice, as a constant companion to call him through sound to pray, night and day.

The Wingless Fairy

A T A YOUNG AGE, I DEVELOPED AN ODD form of stage fright which seeped into my psyche and has remained with me to this day. Indeed I am not altogether sure that I will ever be rid of it. Surely it had its roots in an experience from boarding school.

There was an unwritten, unspoken rule in our secondary school that lead parts in the annual operettas were always reserved for seniors. No girl under sixteen was ever assigned to a principal role. But all that was about to change when I was thirteen. One night Sr Rumold stole into my dormitory cubicle to announce: 'You have been chosen for the part of "Iolanthe" in the opera coming up.' I hadn't the faintest idea of the significance of it all. I just replied, 'Well, sure, why not!'

By the time the curtain went up on our week of performances, I was being hailed as the star of the show. But the final performance, a Saturday matinee, was to burden my soul for many years to come. It was from then on that I felt I had to shroud my voice in a huggermugger silence that lingers to this day. This afternoon performance was the highlight of the school year as it was attended by the local art impresario, critic and playwright, Sir Tyrone Guthrie and his wife, Lady Guthrie. (It is particularly poignant for me to be remembering this moment right now, as I write today in the Guthries' former home at Annaghmakerrig, which, thanks to their generosity and vision, is now an artist's retreat.) During the Overture, the nymphs and their queen Iolanthe are crouched like athletes, ready and waiting to spring up during the first chorus. We listened out, underneath the stage, for the summons of the orchestra to arise and come forth, singing, *'Tripping hither, tripping thither, nobody knows how or whether, we will dance and we will sing, round about our fairy ring'*. With horror, I suddenly realised that I had left my silk wings back on my dormitory bed so that when we appear, I, the principal fairywoman, am wingless!

The nun in charge of the choreography was furious, although I'm sure that neither the Guthries nor anyone else in the audience noticed it at all. I had spoiled her moment in the sun. 'Where is Noreen Ryan?' she hissed during the interval. When I appeared, she slapped me twice on the face and said, 'You couldn't even remember your wings – you'll never do anything properly'. The second half of the operetta is now a total blank for me, and I know that I only managed to sing and finish through the grace of a higher presence within me.

All day Sunday, I was quiet. But on Monday, at a domestic science and biology class, the first effects of that traumatic moment visited me. We gathered together, after elevenses, in the kitchen, which also converted into a science lab when required. Sr Euphemia had us read from our biology book. 'Now, Noreen Ryan', she ordered. I opened my mouth and found that a debilitating stammer had crept into my speech. Dis-

mayed looks from herself and my classmates, but with a
sense of compassion and understanding, at the sudden-
ness, the strangeness of my faltering voice allowed me to
burst into tears. A lovely friend, Frances, was sitting to
my right and I sensed her concern. I put my hand on her
knee, and instinctively she continued reading. I was
grateful for that, and for the next few weeks Sr
Euphemia had the silent sensitivity to leave me be until
the storm had passed.

Two years later, the genre of operetta gave way to
the straight play of 'The Barretts of Wimpole Street'.
Elizabeth Browning's brother, Octavious, 'Ba', has a stut-
ter, and although the plague had left me many months
earlier, having experienced firsthand the sound of the
stuttering state, I carried the role off to perfection, even
to the praise of that same face-slapping sister.

Two Paintings – Two Friends

THE GNAWING ACCEPTANCE THAT I was unpopular made me withdraw further into myself. I would spend hours up in the little music room on the other side of the church gallery corridor. No one noticed my absence, presuming that I was practising my piano and singing. In this tiny haven were two paintings that caught my imagination so deeply that I can recall them in my mind's eye in an instant. The first was 'The Annunciation' by the Dominican painter Fra Angelico; the second was 'The Return of the Prodigal Son' by the Dutch painter and etcher, Rembrandt.

'The Annunciation' hung over the piano and had a discreet gold disc naming title and artist fastened to the dark wooden frame. I would often gaze up at it, weary from the monotony of practising my scales, and daydream about what this moment of surprise and excitement, when the angel announced Mary's miraculous fate if she can but consent, must have been like for her. A supreme aural instant in history, this renowned painting is a hearing icon too; angel and Mary incline their ears to one another out of the arid silence of their salutary hand gestures. Mary welcomes the Angel into the stillness of her home, which is now transformed into the house of 'silent music'. Before our eyes there is a whole chorus of silent joy, anticipating the miraculous arrival of the just conceived Christ – a little one destined to silence the deafening noise of every generation through his endless song of praise, a song that can never be unsung because it has a life and source of its own beyond our own reality. God is the word which enhances and communicates the song of Christ. If we humans were ever to become frozen and silent, the very trees, even the stones, the entire cosmic family on earth would still be able to recall the memory of this song for us. For there is a 'breathing space' between sound and silence; an opportunity to breath in and out easily and in time; to break into the rest, the pause, between the sound of God and God's own silence.

The second painting, Rembrandt's classic, 'The Return of the Prodigal Son', was on the wall to the right of the piano. But it was nameless and frameless, and it wasn't until years later that I fully understood its meaning. Unlike the sweetness of the Annunciation duet, this was a sorrowful duo that somehow reflected and comforted me in my own separation from my father and mother. I was simply drawn to the nourishing message of the loving relationship so gently represented. The older man has his eyes closed so that he can listen all the more intently to his child, I believed. I often cried and prayed that someone too might listen to me and mind me.

Of course, this stretch of time with the St Louis sisters was not without its other graced moments of discovery of another inner world to creativity and blessing. A French-founded order, these women were famous for their commitment, their dedication to the arts, and in so many ways I was blessed to have been sent to study under their care. My singing and piano skills flourished under Mother Francis, and I experienced my homecoming to Western classical music. Once a week we had an optional musical appreciation evening with Sr Marie Christine. I was always first in and last out, so I was often on my own with her. In those moments she would share with me her passion for two composers, Edvard Grieg and Franz Joseph Haydn. In no time they became my darlings too.

Sr De La Salle encouraged me to express myself verbally through debating. She was a genius with words and I learned so much from listening to her seamless flow of speech. She appointed me head of the debating society in my fourth and fifth year, and was an adult *anam chara*, or *anam mhúinteoir* (soul teacher), for those two years. She was also school librarian, and I loved helping her place the returns to their rightful shelves. One evening in sixth year, I felt comfortable enough with her to share how I loved inventing new words when old ones just don't fit or suit their purpose. We must have spent at least an hour inventing new words and new sounds together. 'Why aren't fingers on your hands not called hingers, and toes on your feet not called foes,' I asked her. How often have you been asked to 'pull the door behind you?' I had been at the dentist over the Halloween break, I told her, and the receptionist greeted me with the senseless invitation to 'take a chair in the waiting room'. How is it that much of what we say has no literal meaning and keeps us distanced from one another and from really listening to one another? Although Sr De La Salle was well aware of all the complex linguistic and philosophical issues that I was clumsily staggering upon, she held her peace and listened patiently to me. But she did alert me at that early age to the deeper meanings of language, the metaphorical world where words were beyond the literal and in the realm of the poetic which is God-language, theology. The bottom line is that all language is elastic, flexible and having the property of reshaping in all contexts.

Little did I know then that impulses from the ear's primary hearing centres reach the brain's main language centre, the left hemisphere, where similarly sounding words are converted into logically understood sentences and meaningful thought. Processed through this left half of the cerebrum, the brain hears, for example, the sound 'soul', which sounds exactly like 'sole' (only), 'sole' (fish) and 'Seoul', and always knows the appropriate meaning. It is at this mysterious stage that similarly sounding words are converted into meaningful thought and sentences are understood logically.

Down in the diving bell of all writing, indeed all verbal expression, is the fundamental problem of the limitations of language. Yet the paradox is that it is our only means of expressing our deepest thoughts and experiences of the human and the Divine in our lives. God-talk, which is theology, is a particularly touching example because there seems to be no one word in the world which adequately describes God's powerful presence. But there are some sounds and words that embody the Divine, and the ear is particularly good at tuning into them.

As the bell went for supper that evening, Sr De La Salle just had time to tell me a story that proved the point of how language can fall short of communication or reality.

A very overweight man goes to his doctor for some advice about dieting. 'I have the perfect diet for you now,' said the doctor. 'Just follow the food intake on this sheet for two days, and then skip a day. Come back to me in two weeks and we'll see how you are doing.' Two weeks later, the patient, a shadow of his former self, shows up for his appointment to an incredulous doctor, who gasped, 'My goodness, what happened you? You couldn't have lost such a huge amount of weight on my diet. Did you not follow the instructions I gave you?' 'Oh Lord, I did,' he replied, 'but the damned skipping for a day nearly killed me!'

We both collapsed in uproarious laughter, for which my teacher/friend was apparently later severely reprimanded by some of her superiors, en route to the evening meal.

Twenty-five years later, I reminded Sr De La Salle of this moment when, by the will of the Holy Spirit, we were both living in Boston. She had reclaimed both her lay name, Anne Breslin, and her stylish sense of dress after so many years of wearing a habit. Now she was a highly respected theologian. It was a wonderful reconnection; all the veils, literally and metaphorically, were lifted and we got to know and value one another as equals. She was present for every concert I gave there and I sat in on all her public lectures, listening as avidly then to every word as I did as a teenage student. Shortly after, she was diagnosed with cancer, and some twelve months later I sang at the funeral of this great goddess in the familiar boarding school chapel where I had spent so much time in solitary whisperings with the Divine. She had been a treasured inspiration to so many of her women friends present. Later that evening, we arranged her coffin with the head towards the altar, a position reserved only for an ordained priest. Nobody noticed, or if they did, they remained silent.

THE GOLDEN COUPLE. My parents' wedding photo, 1942.

THE MARIAN-YEAR HOME. Mount Marian, with myself, my brother Noel, and my father standing outside, 1955 (top). L–R: My sister Marion, me, my father, Noel and my mother (above).

With Noel and Marion (top). With Auntie Mai, outside
Mount Marian. I am four and holding a gift of a book from
her (can't see the title but it has to be holy!) (above).

WITH A SONG IN MY HEART. Féile Luimní, when I won the over-fourteen competition at the age of eleven (top). The Wingless Fairy: as 'Iolanthe' at the age of fourteen, three years later, third row, sixth from left (above).

Dún Lughaidh music-room listeners. 'The Annunciation' by Fra Angelico, c. 1440 (top). 'The Return of the Prodigal Son' by Rembrandt Harmenszoon van Rijn, c. 1669 (above).

Pilib Ó Laoghaire, the Cór Cois Laoi choir conductor, from a photo taken in the 1940s (top). With Brendan Kennelly in 1988 at the launch of *Stór Amhrán*, a book of music inspired by Pilib (above).

'THE EAR OF THE HEART' –
BY DEGREES! Kitty's darlings
graduating in 1972 with a
B.Mus.; Mícheál and I, back row
right (top). With proud Ma and
Da (above). MA Supervisor,
Professor Aloys Fleischmann,
with graduate, 1980 (right).

Me in 1986 (above). The
Dungarvan Plainchanters
(1975) (right).

SECOND MOVEMENT
Nourishing the Ear
of the Heart

THEME FOURTEEN

From Law to Freedom at UCC

A T THE END OF THAT SIXTH YEAR, I WAS the only student to present for music as a Leaving Certificate subject. The examination entailed a written paper in June and a practical performance piece three months prior to that, in April. I had no vision of pursuing a musical career. My parents, particularly my mother, would never have entertained the idea because 'it is not pensionable and every lady (like yourself and myself, she added) has to consider this'.

I prayed unceasingly before that 'practical'. 'Ask and you shall receive.' Could I be allocated an ally that would understand? That April morning, as I nervously sat in the practice room awaiting the Department of Education examiner, my two paintings were there for me. I felt their help and support. They alone had heard me play at my best and knew that I could do it.

An elderly, gangly, sharp-featured man with receding grey hair was escorted into the room by Sr Benedict. Pilib Ó Laoghaire terrified me from the start. Coughing incessantly, I could sense from the way in which he opened his briefcase that his fingers, visibly distorted, indeed his whole being, were riddled with pain. I played and sang for him, and did he listen carefully to me! 'What are you doing next year, Nor?' was his

67

very first question. I had never been called 'Nor' before, but I loved the sound of it and instantly all fears were cleared from my mind. An easy one, already well answered. 'Oh, Law in UCD,' I replied. 'You're not, Nor, you're going to come to the university in Cork where I lecture. I will loan you all my books, teach you to conduct choirs and orchestras and you will also be a soprano in my choir (the celebrated Cór Cois Laoi).' 'But my parents won't hear of it,' I lisped. 'No problem,' he replied. 'I'll deal with them.' And that he did. Returning to Cork from Dundalk, he called into Mount Marian, had an extended chat with them, stayed the night, and the deed was done.

Although Ma was sceptical of Pilib's vision for me at first, she drove me down to his home in Cork to talk things through one July day in 1967. We drew into the avenue of his bungalow in Bishopstown. Pilib's elegant wife, Eileen, shyly greeted us and showed us into the front room, a room that, unknowingly then, was to be a crucial listening acoustic chamber for many years to come. Eventually Pilib came in. Minutes later, Eileen arrived in with tea, homemade scones and her speciality, marmalade tart.

I had not seen Pilib since that nerve-racking spring day in Dún Lughaidh four months earlier, all in an April morning, but now I felt completely at ease with him. Soon enough so did Ma, I think. He did all the talking and we took note. That afternoon was a delight for my ears. He spoke proudly of his choir, Cór Cois Laoi, and even played us a tape of them singing at the Cork Choral Festival that May. The song-poem that he played, 'Sheep and Lambs: All in the April Evening', written by the Dublin poet, Katherine Tynan, has walked with me since. I was enthralled at the possibility of finding my own voice, which I did, as his choir member. He took his treasured two-volume copy of *The Grove Dictionary of Music and Musicians* from the bookshelf and promised that I could have it anytime I wished. But that afternoon he made no mention about the greatest 'pearl', as he called it one time, with which he would endow me – the art, the magic, the mystery of *sean-nós* singing.

Mother still insisted that a Bachelor of Music would not guarantee a pensionable career, so a compromise was agreed upon between these two formidable people. I would undertake a Bachelor of Arts degree at University College Cork with Music as one subject only. And so Pilib did do all and much more than he promised. He was an enriching, although far from easy, fount of love and learning. I would never have entered, experienced or felt this third-level world of song, story and choirs without Pilib Ó Laoghaire.

One evening, as we travelled back through Cork city after a choir rehearsal, he firmly suggested, indeed insisted, that I should learn some *sean-nós* songs from him. In his youth, Pilib had been a peripatetic (travelling) Irish school teacher in the beautiful Gaeltacht area of An Rinn, Co. Waterford. Days and nights spent there in the midst of these gifted people, he collected a significant repertoire of old songs and now, with a loving heart, he was passing them on to me.

For months to follow, every Saturday morning I made my way on the Number 11 bus to Bishopstown for my 10 a.m. *sean-nós* lesson. Often tardy, he christened me 'the late Nor'! Initially, I found these songs, the language and the singing style foreign and unfriendly, but I came to seriously respect and revere these traditional jewels.

One particular song, '*Seacht nDólás na Maighdine Muire*' (The Seven Sorrows of Mary), came so easily and naturally that my singing of it took us both by surprise. For Pilib, it carried its own story. Many, many years before, he had been staying in the Caherdaniel townland in the Uíbh Ráthach Gaeltacht of Kerry. After supper in his lodgings, the precious custom was to kneel down, elbows on the seat of the chair, head bowed, to say the Rosary with the family. The *bean an tí*, Bean Uí Dhomhnaill, always brought the circle of fifty Hail Marys to a close by singing these seven sorrows of Mary. After one week there, Pilib, their lodger, had it off by heart.

As he passed this religious carol to me, it somehow awoke an eternal place in the soul that was pure prayer. In reverence and respect to the source, I still sing it to complete my own daily Rosary cycle. The sound of this 'numerical carol' – as it is called in musicology, simply because it recalls a number, in this case the magical figure of seven episodes of the life of Christ – contains a power that wakens what is divine in singer and listener alike.

I really never thanked Pilib Ó Laoghaire for all that he did for me before he passed over on 30 May 1976. Although strangely, the night before I heard the bleak word of his death, some strain of thanksgiving came over me. Spending some time in the Kerry Gaeltacht of Baile an Fheirtéaraigh, I awoke in the middle of the night, alert to a mysterious calling in my dream. Out of the bed, into the kitchen, I started to transcribe, to commit to silent stave, that same Rosary song that was singing in my ear in the dead of the night. It was absolutely vital for me to capture every ornament and contain it within the visual five lines and four spaces of Western classical notation. Doing so helps us to glimpse another face of the song and frees the outsider to awaken its mystery and power.

On hearing of his death that morning, I made the decision that whatever else befalls, I would honour his memory with a book of the *sean-nós* pearls with which he had showered me. These songs, carefully guarded in Pilib's soul, would, like that same soul, never die or be lonely for a singer if they were captured on musical score. *Stór Amhrán*, a book and CD dedicated to Pilib's four children, Colm, Íde, Gearóid and Tadhg, was published in 1988 and republished in 2007.

I sang 'Seacht nDólás na Maighdine Muire' at the outset of the Dublin launch of *Stór Amhrán*, both as a tribute to Pilib and as a blessing on the work. Then poet, Brendan Kennelly, formally sealed the launch, with this to say about the singer and the song:

> Nóirín's special magic springs from her ability to meditate coherently on the nature and consequences of her own passion for music, song and chant. She is a very conscious artist who has a direct, articulate link with her unconscious powers. The beautiful clarity of her singing and her thinking is born of her intrepid ability to confront and express the complexity of her dreams, instincts, aspirations and longings. I believe that is why her genius, at once contained and soaring, creates in the listener's heart an atmosphere of serenity and calm ... True music of the spirit.

Seán Ó Riada –
The First of the 'John Quartet'

MY FIRST MEMORIES OF UNIVERSITY College Cork are of the now legendary composer, Seán Ó Riada. At the age of sixteen, I was waiting to audition for a place in the Music Department. The secretary led me up the stairs and, desperately nervous, I waited outside the music room in the dark corridor. Aloys Fleischmann, the professor of the department, appeared, dressed impeccably in a pin-striped navy suit and bright red tie, and called out, 'Next is Miss Ryan'. Down the steps I went, and once inside the wood-panelled room, Professor Fleischmann looked out over his thick, black-rimmed glasses at me and said, 'This is Mister Ó *Reeuhduh*'. As I shook Seán's hand for the first time and caught his eye, I recognised a helper somehow. The professor pointed to the piano and I played a Bach Prelude so badly that I knew the Prof (as we were later to call Professor Fleischmann) was in pain! But Seán was smiling. I would love to have been a fly on that wood-panelled wall to have heard the conversation that ensued! At any rate, I was offered a place in the Music Department at UCC the next month.

Seán Ó Riada, 'Johnny Reidy', knew the art of story-telling well. He could project the sound of the story all around our dark, wooden lecture room, as he did one November afternoon. First Arts Music students were not as serious a consideration or as great a responsibility as music students per se. Seán was aware of this. At our 4 p.m. lecture with him on musical form, with a glint in his eye, he whispered to us, 'I just heard a great story about a song! Would you like to hear it?' Of course, the reply was 'yes'.

'Once upon a time, there was a rare bird called "Rary",' he began. For forty minutes, we remained spellbound; his jovial, melodious voice resonated and harmonised with our souls in a far deeper way than any counterpoint (the art of combining melodies, which he had been scheduled to teach us that day) ever could. We hung upon his every word, following the wild escapades of this exotic, unfortunate bird. Rary comes to his final destination, followed in hot pursuit by his enemies, who are seeking to destroy him. In despair, overlooking the cliff's edge onto the raging sea below, Rary looked back at his enemy pursuers, and sang, '*It's a long way to tip a rary*'!

One time when I was in the United States, the memory of that 'rary' bird re-visited me. I was in a taxi in Berkeley, California, and the cab driver asked me where I was from. Living in Co. Tipperary at the time, I said, 'Oh, from Ireland, Tipperary actually, as in (I then broke into song) "*It's a long way to Tipperary*"'! 'Wow!' he replied, 'I always thought that was an American cowboy song – "*It's a long way to de prairie*"! What d'ya know, ma'am, you hear something new every day!' And it's true!

One freezing Monday morning, around Christmas, there was no sign of Seán Ó for our contemporary music class. This was not an uncommon occurrence. Eventually he breezed in, dishevelled, clad in a three-piece tweed suit with green tweed tie, evidently just returning from one of his exotic international gatherings in Dublin. Smiling cunningly, he invited us to come to the wonderful bay window at the back of the room to observe his latest acquisition. We did and gasped when we saw a red Mercedes car down below. He was very proud of it.

That morning, he sat at the piano and played a series of improvisations on a Christmas song, 'The Wexford Carol'. We were aware then that this was going to be a blessed moment of inspiration. Mesmerised, we listened as he musically turned the tune upside down and inside out. The artfulness of improvisation was awoken in our hearts that very morning. Years later, reading a Zen story, I realised that the enlightenment, the improvisational epiphany for us that morning, is perfectly described here:

> A mother takes her five-year-old daughter to the studio of a sculptor who is busily chiselling a huge slab of marble in the middle of the room. Two weeks later, the two return, and on entering the studio see the black marble figure of a male lion, with perfectly sculpted limbs and mane, its two ears poised to hear. The little girl runs up to the sculptor and in a little high-pitched voice exclaims: 'How did you know he was in there?'

That was the extraordinary dexterity of Ó Riada: he
could sculpt a symphony out of one little note.

Aristotle held that all education was about turning
the soul of the learners towards the good, the true and the
beautiful. Seán was a true educator, leading us to levels
of listening awareness that we never knew were there,
forever rotating our souls to magnificence. During one
contemporary music class, he introduced us to an iconic
figure whose breath of presence surpassed all others, the
then living American composer, John Cage, who was
later to become a real presence in my life. 'Listen carefully
to this piece of music,' Seán said. He placed a vinyl LP on
the record player. 'I've just got this from the land of the
brave and the free,' he added, with a deliberate, far-away
look on his handsome, angular face. I enquired about
the title of the piece. Seán scribbled 4.33 on the black-
board and I somehow knew that he was once again
about to bestow an experience on us that would shape
the rest of our lives.

Seán sat down at the mahogany desk at the top of
the room, staring at us with an impish grin as we
listened intently. At first, no discernible sound at all, let
alone music, came from the machine. Then the odd
cough from a faraway audience, irregular shuffles and
noises blended with our own giggles and discomfort as
we listened in the strange silence for the time duration
of the title.

Although I do not recall Seán's precise words, we all
knew the wonder, the awe that our own John held for
this other John. 'The soul selects her own society', as
Emily Dickinson says in six words what the Irish
proverb celebrates in four: '*Aithníonn ciaróg, ciaróg eile*'
(one spider recognises another).

NÓIRÍN
NÍ RIAIN

My concept of silence and the world was enlarged and challenged over that four and a half minutes' listening. Up till then, I had a terror of the white space of silence. I knew that Cage's gift had much more to offer my religious experience than my musical education. The ear of my heart was transformed by the power of the listening silence to shatter the walls and barriers of disbelief. Seán explained that Cage sought to eliminate the marked distinction between 'art', the 'concert-hall' and 'being' and 'living'.

Out of the debate that ensued on the piece, I first celebrated, and have done so since, the gift, physically and spiritually, of the ambience of absence of sound. You see, Cage's work of art proves that an ambience of complete absence of sound is impossible to create and sustain. The listening ear is never silent – it is open to the myriad sonic demands all around.

Silence and sound create an inseparable duality. Thus, stillness and its corresponding resonance simply 'are'. Silence is the *cantus firmus* of life; the steady, regular life-force to which all our true experiences are melodiously added. All sound merely interacts with the constant vibrating silent hue of nature. Silence can also be the heart of the soul that reveals the friendship with oneself. The ancient Chinese proverb, 'The sound ceases but the sense goes on', summarises true silence. A listening in the silence is irretrievable, yet crystal clear. According to Seamus Heaney, the 'silence breathed / and could not settle back'.[5]

5. Heaney, 'Station Island', *Station Island*, Faber and Faber, 1985, p. 61.

Eastern spiritualities have so much to teach us about silence. No doubt that John Cage's fascination with Zen Buddhism (about which I heard him speak so passionately twenty years later) sculpted the inspiration for this controversial piece, all about our capacity for really being in the 'here/hear and now'.

There and then, '4.33' opened my ears to understanding the distinction to be made between first-hand and second-hand, even first-ear and second-ear hearing. The first-ear experience of being in physical ear-shot during a concert has more forceful intensity than the second-ear experience of listening to a recording, where the power ceases to exist or is at least greatly diminished. Listening 'live' (even that word is significant) to someone, music, or cosmic sounds, always holds everything together in perfect unity. Disembodied listening is a shabby substitute for the real thing.

No two listenings or tuning-ins to Cage's silence are identical. The praying/listening moment changes each time and is different for everyone. One must become comfortable in the improvisatory silence, that is, a silence that is on the spur of the moment, open and free to the stirrings of the Holy Spirit. Simply, it is playing silence by ear.

This piece from John Cage was a great lesson for me in the schoolroom about a stillness that can be the grace of God freely and lovingly bestowed. According to Thomas Carlyle, 'Speech is of time, silence is of eternity'. The theological overtones are both on an aural and a silent level: being present to the sound and the silence which reveal God is being present to the actual moment which is not disembodied.

No two silent listenings to the inner voice of God's self-disclosure are the same either. The God who freely reveals will be known not only in names but also in silence. This silence does not reduce God to absence or mere emptiness, but is fullness, which is a Trinity of

Persons. It is almost as if the Trinity is not composed of just three parts but of four: the fourth is the silence that reveals the triune God to the universe and wherein cosmic sound disappears into the silent mist. Human silence, which human ears can perceive, arises out of the silence that cannot be heard, yet which is drawn back to the world by an organic momentum. The Word is the fruit of the silent seed of Divine/human encounter. To taste the full fruit is to taste the revelation of God in and through the dialogical Trinity. Silence is a pair of bookends: one is placed at each end of the Two Testaments of Scripture, holding upright and together the silent message of *Deus Semper Major* (God is always more).

Another gift which Ó Riada extended to us with such beauty, elegance and reverence was the treasure trove of the Irish language. We welcomed this new insight, this revelation with bright delight. We were being marvellously prepared for Divine language because we knew the sounds of this other-world vocabulary. We were captivated by the mystical, magical sound of the Irish language as Seán spoke it and about it. Before meeting Seán Ó, we viewed Irish as a chore, something that had to be studied and learned, and we were in no way *líofa* (fluent). Fired by his linguistic spell over us, we soon became fervent, natural Irish language lovers.

⁓

The lodgings assigned to me by the accommodations office for my first two university years were certainly guided by some guarding force and were a pure blessing. From the sound and meaning of the address, 'Cill Dara' – the church of the oak – my heart felt at home there, just as I had always felt midst the oak trees of Glenstal Abbey. I received a great sense of relationship and listening from Bríd, the *bean an tí*, and her husband, Seán Seosamh, the *fear an tí*, who was a glorious, gifted storyteller. He worked daily in a drapery shop, and at night-time would regale Bríd and I, their young student, with the most outrageous of stories. During my first weeks, he lost me on two counts: the speedy pace of his speaking, and the newness of the sound of his lilting Cork accent. But his easy way with blending surprise, sound and story was as important for me as all that I was hearing and learning about music during the academic day. Storytelling is all about sound and this was one powerful gift that Seosamh passed on to me. I hope that I have never lost it and that I can teach it to others too.

This young couple shaped my horizon of love and belonging. I longed and prayed in the little front bedroom of their semi-detached house for the depth and ease of their connection for myself at some stage. And just one year later, that raggle-taggle reality appeared.

Theme Sixteen

Anam Chara – Michael O'Sullivan … Kitty, Grieg and Haydn

I COMPLETED MY FIRST YEAR AS A BA STUDENT, studying English, Philosophy, Sociology and Music, in 1968. Although I just barely scraped through the first three, my music results were first honours. My parents eventually listened to the Ó Laoghairian voice of reason and agreed to let me study music full time.

A new venue for the Music Department, the Rectory, awaited us, and it was all very exciting that first autumnal afternoon when we assembled. 'My God,' the secretary whispered to the five of us female veterans who had been with her the previous year, 'there are twenty-two of you in First Year Music, eleven boys and eleven girls. That has never happened before, you know! Always lots of girls and very few lads. But you, girls, are my hens of the walk, and I have a task for each of you. Noreen, will you go to the top of the stairs and direct the new people to the main lecture room?'

First up was a gangly, smiling fair-haired lad clad in a yellow and red silk necktie that was at odds with his fashionable Beatle boots. He held out his right hand to me. 'I'm Michael O'Sullivan.' And that was it. The initial sound of his voice rang a bell not of prior memory but of future soul connection. I slipped into my lecture room place beside my two good friends from the previous year and whispered, 'Well there's at least one lovely fella in the class, anyway'. From that evening on, I had a new intention for my Cill Dara prayers.

A few months later we were the natural couple of the Rectory. Although the Prof often shook his index finger at us as we emerged from the pictures in Montenotte, near his home, he as often smiled down at us in approval at his concerts in Dublin and Cork.

We were for many, many years joined in some ancient, primal, sacred world of belonging and mutual understanding. We shared our innermost thoughts and feelings in a bond of friendship that reached way beyond convention and definition. After hearing us on a radio programme in 1979, *Irish Press* journalist Mary Lappin had this to say: 'A fascinating interview with Nóirín Ní Riain and Mícheál Ó Súilleabháin established that the husband and wife team is as well versed in verbal as in musical communication ... it was a formidable fusion of scholarship and executive ability. If they are not the best informed and most musical duo in these islands, the competition has yet to present itself.'[6]

Those were halcyon days at University College Cork. (Sr De La Salle, from my Dún Lughaidh days, is my source for this term. A great admirer of my singing, she once told me that I was like a 'halcyon bird': a kingfisher singing bird who, according to ancient Greek legend, breeds around the time of the winter Solstice in a nest floating on a troubled sea. In and through the beautiful sound of its singing song the seas are calmed

6. *Irish Press*, 21/04/79.

and charmed into stillness.) Apart from falling in love with my future husband, I fell in love with the Honan Church – the natural threshold between the Glenstal Church and the chapel in Dundalk. The magnificent beauty of all the stained-glass windows, particularly the windows of Sarah Purser and Harry Clarke, are luminous icons that astound the eye of the beholder. Then there is the winding mosaic river-run floor. Every stone of that chapel spoke to me. Very soon, I sought out the day-to-day running of the chaplaincy. I was a 'Jill of all trades': setting up the altar – fulfilling my youthful desire to be an altar boy after all – and even occasionally playing the organ. I read the Scripture and sang psalms. When anyone suggested meeting up with me, including Mick, I cajoled them into meeting me there after midday Mass.

Our class was a rather conscientious lot, so we valued any unstructured time amongst ourselves. We, eleven boys and eleven girls, were a maverick, exceptional gathering. We became almost a monastic community, learning, singing, eating together daily.

The Rectory cleaner, Kitty, a true Corkonian, adopted us and let us into her basement kitchen for endless cups of tea. We would crowd in there at every free moment and out would come tin whistles and fiddles. Out too came the voices, and we listened and sang out of our hearts there, with Kitty all ears.

Once, we hustled her into a bus bound for the Opera Festival in Dublin. Verdi's 'A Masked Ball' was the programme. 'Well Mick and Nor,' she sighed on our way back, 'I never heard the likes of such screechin.' Sure I'd much rather be listening to ye in me oul kitchen any day.'

82

One frosty winter morning, she told me that she'd
slept it in and missed her daily morning Mass. I gently
suggested that she might come up to the Honan Mass
at noon, and she did. For her, the statues moved her far
more than my mere mortal song ever could do: 'You
sang great, Nor, but, d'ye know, them statues are beautiful. They never sing at all; they just stand there in
silence. I wonder what they'd say if they could speak?'

One of the most enduring memories from that time is
of a practical examination I had. Having performed a
portfolio of classical songs, I then had to sit before the
board for a *viva voce*. (I have always loved those two
Latin words, the meaning of them too – 'with the living
voice'.) The first question Professor Fleischmann
asked, to put me at ease and to activate my own vibrant
sound, was simply, 'What genre of songs do you like
best?' No hesitancy, I casually replied, 'Oh, Western
classical music – Edvard Grieg and Franz Joseph Haydn,
the two voices that have blended my second and third
level education.' I should have left it at that but I
prattled on. 'Well, actually, their styles are very similar.'

'Oh Miss Ni *Reehun*, what an extraordinary thing to
say,' the Prof exclaimed. Somehow I found the words to
argue my case. Later, a lecturer who had been present
told me in confidence that it was this original stance
had decided the examiners to award me an honours
rather than a pass. The moral of this vignette is that the
Holy Spirit herself recognises the innocent enthusiasm
that allows you to make the most irrational claims and
waits with you as you hem and haw through limp argu-
ments, which do eventually, miraculously, convince
the startled listener.

83

'Keep a Green Tree in Your Heart and Some Day a Singing Bird will Nest There'[7]

7. Ancient Chinese proverb.

I LEARNED A LOT ABOUT WESTERN CLASSICAL singing in university, but was in doubt about whether I could say 'Amen' (the Hebrew for 'So be it' or 'Let it be') to it all. In ways, this singing technique has often tried to work against the natural God-given voice. My own experience is living proof of this. Two weeks before my final singing diploma examination in 1970, after I had practised for hours and hours, I heard my three Diploma colleagues singing their hearts out nearby in preparation too. We were all singing in exactly the same timbre: a highly technical, developed sound taught to us by the same voice mistress. Nothing wrong with this, one could argue; our voice mentor was a very competent exponent and transmitter of that style, which does tend to stereotype the voice. (A respected voice therapist, Paul Newham, suggests that in European classical singing, 'the aim ... has always been to reduce or even eliminate the changes in timbre between one register and another'.)[8]

8. Newham, *The Singing Cure*, Shambhala, 1994, p. 125.

84

But at that particular moment of hearing, I realised that I was a vocal imposter, acting out a voice-role that was not the entire me. There was falseness for me in the technique, which lacked poise and sacred light, and I was uncomfortable hearing it. I recognised that this was not the voice that God wanted me to sing in. Next morning at my singing lesson, I decided to share this with our teacher, suggesting that the true grain of my voice was a symbiosis, a mélange, a blend of *sean-nós*, traditional style, plainchant and classical technique. Could I find, with her help, my true voice and sound? She was shocked, particularly at the suggestion of introducing *sean-nós*. 'That's just singing through your nose, by ear,' she replied! Two no-go areas for any classical singer. Not only did she refuse to dialogue, but she forbade me from carrying out the examination, and furthermore withdrew access to the appointed accompanist. Undaunted, though deeply hurt, I soldiered on and a lovely friend offered to accompany me for that crucial examination. Like a wounded bird, I sang from the depths of my heart and was awarded the highest marks of all four of us. The singing bird did come and nest.

Sean-Nós, Mé-Féin Nós[9]

URING THAT INSPIRATIONAL Ó RIADA awakening to the beauty of Irish, and learning to trust the love between us, Mick and I hit out for the Gaeltacht of Chorca Dhuibhne, Kerry, in the summer of 1971 for an immersion course in Irish and, of course, in our new-found love.

Off the bus at An Gráig, we were first up to the door of our *lóistín* (lodgings). Out came the *fear an tí*, his weathered, swarthy good-looking face wrinkled like a matured walnut. *'Cad is ainm duit?'*, he asked. 'Noreen Ryan,' I answered. I hadn't the wisdom to respond in Irish. He looked out in the direction of the Blasket Islands and said, *'Oh, muise, "Nóirín Ní Riain" is ainm duit anois, a chailín, agus ná baic le teanga mhadra as seo amach.'* ('Nóirín Ní Riain' is your name now, girleen, and don't bother with the dog's language from now on!) His sounding of my name was the be all and end all – the Amen. Saint Augustine had it right on this one – 'Singing "Amen" is like singing your own name,' he claimed. From then on, I was totally committed to 'Nóirín Ní Riain'.

We could hardly wait every evening of that fortnight to step it out to Tig Kruger's where, alcohol free, we were intoxicated with the sound of *sean-nós* singing.

That's where we first met Seán de hÓra, the local legendary singer, and keenly observing him I was alerted to
that breath-taking moment before a traditional singer
breaks the silence. For me this was remarkably surprising and exciting. In the breathing space between the
motion and rest of inhaling and exhaling, Seán would
prepare the entire body to birth the song. The gestation period being fulfilled, the first sound is out and
everyone cheers. The song is turned out; the breathing
space is born.

The Parable of the Singer by the nineteenth-century
Scottish novelist and poet, George MacDonald, carefully and unerringly captures such a moment. Every
time I read it aloud, this touching tale always coaxes
me down new pathways of understanding the singer,
the song, the listener and the Divine. There is the
desire to lean forward, ears poised to listen. There is
the longing to become the song, the heroine of the tale.
Then, the ultimate rhythm of the singer emerges at
the entrance of the 'cavern where God weaveth the
garment of souls'. Read on – aloud if you can:

> And lo! Behind me was a great hole in the rock …
> and when I looked into it I shuddered, for I
> thought I saw far down the glimmer of a star.
>
> The youth entered and vanished … I lay in ter-
> ror near the mouth of the vast cavern. When I
> looked up once more, I saw all the men leaning
> forward with head aside, as if listening intently
> to a far-off sound. I likewise listened, but though
> much nearer than they I heard nothing. But I
> could see their faces change like waters in a
> windy and half-cloudy day. Sometimes, though I

87

heard nought, it seemed to me as if one sighed or prayed beside me, and once I heard a clang of music, triumphant in hope; but I looked up, and lo it was the listeners who stood on their feet and sang. They ceased, sat down, and listened as before. At last one approached me, and I ventured to question him. 'Sir,' I said, 'wilt thou tell me what it means!' And he answered me thus. 'This youth desired to sing to the Immortals. It is a law with us that no one shall sing a song who cannot be the hero of his tale, who cannot live the song he sings ... Therefore he enters the cavern where God weaveth the garment of souls, and there he lives in the form of his own dream ... The sighs which thou didst hear were his longings after his own ideal, and thou didst hear him praying for the truth he beheld but could not reach. We sang because in his first battle, he strove well and overcame. We await the next.[10]

10. MacDonald,
*Within and
Without – A
Dramatic Poem*,
Longman,
Brown, Green
and Longmans,
1855, p. 70.

In the Irish tradition, when we asked someone to sing a song, the call is '*Cas amhrán dúinn*'. This literally means 'turn a song for us'. Tradition has it (sadly but a memory now) that when you were invited to 'turn a song', you'd take and gently, timelessly turn and turn again the hand of a listening neighbour seated or standing beside you. The tender circle both of your own hand and the hand held in it in an empathetic palm cycle is a physical accompaniment to the song. Until the sound ceases into silence, the motion is, in Aristotelian terms, to direct the soul of the singer and listener towards the good and the Divine, towards 'the Immortals'. The silent sound waves are interrupted and surprised not only by the song notes but also by the devoted hand gestures. Sound and silence are talking intimately and temporarily in the circle of the two hands; extreme excitement is in the inhalation and expiration. There must be the perfect balance and depth too between breathing in and breathing out.

Around this time when we were wild out about our aural tradition, Mick and I visited our mentor, Seán Ó, at the Bons Secours Hospital in Cork. We'd been warned that he was poorly but were not prepared for his wasted, deathly appearance. He still managed to smile up at us and he was particularly touched to see Mick – the best student he ever had and a genius in his eyes, he once said.

Seán died shortly afterwards, on 3 October 1971. He was just forty, but he managed to touch and enrich the lives of so many and to turn not only our songs but our souls, musically and linguistically, beyond all recognition.

Plainchant – From Waterford to Costa Rica

ARLY DEGREES COMPLETED, THE NEXT step for Mick and me was marriage. Engaged at twenty-two, we were married one year later on 27 June 1974. Drawn yet again by the supreme beauty of the Irish language, we applied for teaching jobs in Dungarvan in the shadow of An Rinn Gaeltacht where we lived. Every morning and evening, we left and returned to our lovely little rented cottage in Cnocán a'Phaoraigh (the Hill of the Powers). Some of the local children befriended us and it was through them that easy-speaking Irish entered our souls. Most evenings after school, these bright little bubbling faces appeared at our bungalow window and out came the orange drinks, *bríoscaí* (biscuits) and the *cúpla focail* (few words).

I spent the year teaching in the girl's secondary school with the warm, motherly Mercy sisters in that Co. Waterford town. I was full of enthusiasm. (I adore that word, which comes from the Greek '*enthous*', out of the sound '*theos*', 'god', and means 'possessed by God'.) Armed and fired by this passionate eagerness and little else, I rushed into the principal's office with my plan. 'Mother Angela, could I listen to every girl in the school – I would like to form a school choir of the finest songbirds among them.' She listened carefully, measuring up the implications for her timetables, before agreeing to give me three forty-minute periods a week with the selected students. Didn't we sing out of our young hearts all that year – those twenty-nine voices that tickled my ears. I was so proud of these talented songsters, and we sang at many school and public events. Just twenty-three years old myself, I was more like their older sister, and my girls confided all their troubles and secrets in me. I taught them almost as many song genres as they numbered: we warbled from classical to jazz, from medieval love songs to *sean-nós*, from rock to plainchant, from simple operatic arias to three-part harmonic arrangements. Somewhere deep down in me, I resolved to encourage and inspire them just at that time in their lives when I myself was unconsciously deprived of empowerment.

During our time together, I always started with a prayer-chant – a Kyrie Eleison, or an Alleluia, or an Amen – to bless the good work of it all. Only much later did I learn from the Rule of St Benedict that to bless new work with a prayer is always a good idea. 'And first of all, whatever good work you begin to do, beg of God with most earnest prayer to perfect it …' We then cantered through a whole range of songs that meant the world to me then. At the end of the school year we had to part company, as Mick had been appointed assistant lecturer in UCC, beginning in October. Thirty hearts were broken!

That final June afternoon we talked about our past year together. 'What did you enjoy singing most?' I tentatively asked. 'Oh, I loved that God stuff,' was the eager response from the rowdiest girl. 'The ordinary chant, you called it.' 'Me too, me too, me too,' piped up the others. I hastily explained that it was called *plain*chant, not ordinary chant, and indeed that there was nothing monotonous or lifeless about it. They were agreed. 'Oh for heaven's sake,' I then exclaimed, 'but you don't even like going to Mass! Why did you like the plainchant so much?' They spent the remainder of the class explaining how they felt happier somehow, more at peace in themselves, after singing this extraordinary, unusual song, although they admitted that they had very little notion of the actual meaning of the words. Somehow it was the sound that mattered and that delighted.

Plainchant is a great Christian communication skill, breaking down language and cultural barricades instantly. I have had many experiences over the years where just being together chanting creates a bond infinitely deeper than any form of words can do.

One spectacular remembrance of instant recognition and fellowship through chant returns regularly. It was in 1989 in Costa Rica at a week-long international interfaith conference. My brief from the University of Peace in San José was to lead His Holiness, the fourteenth Dalai Lama of Tibet, Tenzin Gyatso, in song into the town hall every morning, where he delivered his daily address.

One afternoon, there was a ceremony in an enormous cathedral in Carthago, a nearby village. His Holiness and other world leaders entered behind me as I sang. To the right of the altar in an enclosed space behind the grid barrier were over two hundred young seminarians, who sang some beautiful plainchant

during the hour-long service. When the ceremony was
over, I so wanted to tell them how much I loved their
singing, but I did not speak their Spanish language. In
desperation and frustration, I boldly walked up to the
grille that separated us and self-assuredly intoned one of
the most beautiful chants to the Mother of God,
Regina Caeli. Suddenly the whole choir was joining in
with me, as were many of the locals still gathered in the
church. The physical, psychological, cultural linguistic
fortresses were dissolved instantly through the singing.
Bells in the Cathedral belfry added a descant as they
pealed out over the rainforest, and continued their
hymn of praise long after we had finished our hymn to
Mary begging her to *ora pro nobis Deum, alleluia'* (Pray
for us to God, alleluia).

Over the years I have given many plainchant
workshops, and the power of this song to transfigure
the soul in singers and listeners alike still surprises
me. Once received in the ear of the heart, it never
leaves. At a workshop I gave recently in Co. Meath, we
were mindfully and sensitively singing some Kyrie
Eleisons, Alleluias and other chestnuts from plainchant like Adoro Te and Regina Caeli. Barbara, a
participant in her eighties, excitedly told us how one
particular Kyrie Eleison echoes from her youth, and
how she sings it all the time, out loud, as she mows the
lawn. 'You'd never be thinking badly about anyone
when you're singing that chant! Instead, you'd be
thinking of everybody else and asking God to have pity
on them.' There and then, she burst into the inspired
Kyrie from the aptly named 'Missa de Angelis' (Mass
of the Angels) (recalling my own youthful singing in
Caherline church).

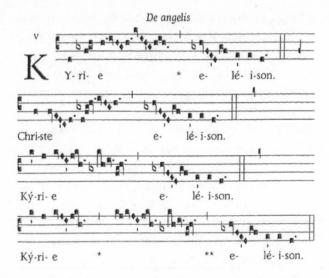

Barbara had not realised until that work/prayer shop moment that these mystical words that she had been singing for years were Greek, not Latin, and furthermore meant, 'Lord, have mercy, Christ, have mercy'! Along with the mysterious meaning, we have lost this gracious repertoire of Kyrie Eleisons in some dark recess of the plainchant treasure chest. These two beautifully sonic Greek invocations, Kyrie Eleison and Christe Eleison, were the cornerstones of early Christian liturgy. This we know from the letters of a Gallican nun, Egeria. She made a pilgrimage to Jerusalem in AD 381, and in her letters back to her convent she describes the liturgies, with particular reference to these gems in the plainchant canon.

Three Kyrie Eleisons, three Christe Eleisons and again three Kyrie Eleisons were originally sung nine times at the outset of the liturgy of the Eucharist. No doubt that it was in honour of the Trinity; one Kyrie

94

for Creator, the son Jesus and Holy Spirit, one Christe
for all three again and a Kyrie again for God, Christ and
Holy Spirit. The final Kyrie to the Holy Spirit is the fine
wine kept until last – the final invocation, the last gasp
to the Divine for help. The music changes to heighten
the very final calling, the ultimate encore for a hearing.
And like any concert encore, the stops are pulled out so
that the listener is swept to their feet for a standing
ovation.

When you sing these prayer chants all nine times,
there is a horizon of timelessness that descends. This
skyline of vocal prayer is at once lost when the ritual is
shortened. The transition from Latin to the vernacular
in the late 1960s rendered these age-old sounds silent.
What a tragedy! Everything around most church worship now is about timing; the quicker the better is the
motto. (Carl Jung once wrote that hurry is not only the
business of the devil, it *is* the devil.)

Mark Patrick Hederman, a dear friend, and abbot
of Glenstal, tells the story of a journey he took in a taxi
from the airport into New York. The cab driver was
playing a CD of plainchant, so, striking up a conversation, Patrick commented, 'That's plainchant'. 'Yes,
yes,' said the driver, 'I play it all the time. My shrink
says that it's great for road rage.'

Glenstal Abbey Revisited

A REPRISE, A RETURN TO MY FIRST connection with Glenstal Abbey, happened in a very organic, personal way in 1976, following our year teaching in Dungarvan. The little church in Caherline where I had sung plainchant many times beside my teacher-mother had just been refurbished and was to be blessed and re-opened. I was invited by the curate as the schoolmistress's daughter and local singer to bless the opening in song. So were the monks of Glenstal Abbey. 'Oh the monks will add a bit of *clawss*,' the curate whispered to me. The same plainchants that Ma had hammered into us twenty years ago in this very space were now familiarly wafting across the altar. Here was I singing some traditional religious songs that I had just taken into my heart. That same year, I began collecting and singing these beautiful *dánta Dé* (poems of God) for a Master's Degree in Music.

At tea afterwards, Mick and I met Dom Paul McDonnell, the Benedictine organist and choirmaster. He told us that he had been a great friend of our mentor, Seán Ó Riada. In fact, he had commissioned Seán's second Mass for Glenstal Abbey. 'Would you consider coming to Glenstal Abbey next Sunday to sing some of it for a nuns' congress?' Dom Paul enquired. Of course

I would, and I did, and that's how the re-connection with this Narnian forest of my youth began. The following week I sang 'A Íosa Bháin' from that Ó Riada Mass, from the lectern that was to behold my shadow and listen to my voice many times over the years to come.

One handsome, blue-eyed monk smiled warmly at us as he left the altar. He was Brother Patrick Hederman, now, as I mentioned, the abbot, but then a young visionary, philosopher monk. That day we also met two other brothers in the community, Ciarán and Simon, who were both about to study in UCC the following year for a Higher Diploma in Education. So for the next year they were regular visitors to our house in Glanmire in Cork.

On that summer's day in Glenstal Abbey, three Benedictine monks entered our lives in a circle of friendship that has been a visible, unbroken and aural grace since. I felt at home in our companionship of five people, belonging as a duo in some way to Glenstal Abbey, all of us searchers and seekers for the presence of the Divine and the temple of the Spirit of belonging, in ourselves and through each other.

⁓

July 25th, 1978, was an important day: I launched my very first recording, *Seinn Aililiú*. This would never have seen the light of day without the vision and support of Mick, who made it all happen by arranging and directing many songs taught to me by Pilib for a 'band' of musicians. It was a laboratory of song exploration, and thankfully it was pleasantly welcomed by most listeners and music critics: 'The album is an elaborate and delightful production ... throught-provoking as well as being good to the ear ... In short, the experiment works, but the crucial factor in its success hinges on the natural beauty and abundant colour of Nóirín Ní Riain's voice.'[11] 'To my ears, Nóirín Ní Riain not only has a lovely voice for the purpose but has a deep knowledge and love of *sean-nós*. I find her singing, her style, her embellishments, her phrasing quite lovely and very moving.'[12]

The album did have its fault-finders too: '... while there are some good moments laced throughout, the music suffers from a lack of decisive direction ... About Nóirín's voice, my own feeling is that it still suffers from the constraints of her training as a classical singer. There's still a tightness of style she'll need to thoroughly undo to be successful as a more contemporary singer ... taken as a whole, its impact is somewhat frustrating.'[13]

11. Bill Meek, *Irish Times*, 29/08/78.

12. Charles Acton, *Irish Times*, 04/09/78.

13. Julian Vignoles, *Hotpress*, 1978.

Dream Time
– From M.A. to Ma

HE YEAR 1980 WAS A VERY CREATIVE one, an annum full of intensity and a youthful sense of adventure. It was a time of preparation and productivity on three fronts: like the liturgical seasons of Advent and Lent – a time of waiting and expectancy – we, after five years of marriage, were expecting the birth of our first son, Eoin Benedict. Just before his arrival I had completed a Masters degree on a classification of tradition religious song in Irish. Also, the source-sound of our friendship between the Benedictine Glenstal Abbey community and ourselves was released in a recording of these same spiritual *sean-nós* songs, *Caoineadh na Maighdine* (The Virgin's Lament).

I had the blessed opportunity to emerge from academia with a Masters Degree from UCC. Choosing the research area of traditional religious song in Irish was logical and inevitable. Learning the elegant '*Seacht nDólás na Maighdine Muire*' from Pilib Ó Laoghaire years before awoke a fascination in me for any traditional Irish spiritual song, an insatiable desire to discover and sing more of the same. I longed to learn about them, to define them musically, historically and poetically, and realised that very little formal research or indeed collecting had been done up to then.

No form of hymnology in Irish existed in Ireland because of the suppression of public Catholic worship in the seventeenth and eighteenth centuries. However, a small rich repertoire of traditional religious folk songs sung at the hearth has survived. This tradition of singing a religious song in the intimate surroundings of the home is in harmony with the Irish advice of the heart: God is not confined to the church but lives and breathes in every single facet of life. The classification of these irresistible religious songs became my mission, and Professor Fleischmann agreed to supervise the thesis.

Although research can sometimes be tedious, I loved every minute of it for at least three reasons: first, these '*dánta Dé*' were deeply personal prayers, devout songs where my imagination found in them the food it had for years been desiring. Second, I realised that adding a layer of sung sound to any words immensely intensifies its meaning and physical effect. I lived and loved the reality that a poem lives only through the sound. The meaning is heightened, not diluted, in the sounding. Third, for the first time too I was fascinated to learn how the ear held court in the early days of our foreparents. Writing and literacy were late acquisitions of the Irish. We were slow to read. The advent and growth of literacy in Ireland is almost exclusively linked to ecclesiastical, monastic scribes and indeed to the advent of Christianity in Ireland. The story-telling aspect of Irish spirituality is present in religious folk song, the major source of Irish spirituality. To be a poet, religious or secular, in early medieval, and even recent

100

Ireland, was to be an expert on the sound of every word of one's poem; a poem got going through the sound of the speaking voice. We Irish are a people of a strong ancient aural, story-telling culture. Since the Christian religion is primarily a religion of the ear, we took to each other as the canyon takes to echo. Ireland's God is aural and oral.

I love the experience and observations of literary historian and anthropologist, Robin Flower. He held that it is in the very act of uttering that the music of the word is heard: 'If the spoken Irish of today is … the liveliest, the most concise, and the most literary in its turns of all vernaculars of Europe, this is due in no small part to the passionate preoccupation of the poets … restlessly seeking the last perfection of phrase and idiom.'[14]

14. Flower, *The Irish Tradition*, Oxford University Press (1947), 1979, p. 106.

One particular moment painted by Flower is forever etched on my soul. He wrote how one day on the Aran Islands in the 1930s, time seemed eternal through the sound of a voice. Quite by chance, he had stumbled on an old man digging potatoes in a field. This octogenarian, as Flower puts it, 'fell to reciting Ossianic lays'. These are an ancient blend of chanted poems and prose in Irish telling mythological tales about Fionn and his exploits in Greece. This lay-reciting tradition has been compared to plainchant in style and performance:

> At times the voice would alter and quicken, the eyes would brighten; as with a speed which you would have thought beyond the compass of human breath, he delivered those passages … full of strange words and alliterating rhetorical

101

15. Ibid., p. 105.

phrases ... I listened spellbound ... a real and vivid experience.[15]

The boundless, improvised style of free verse is probably the most appropriate description of my Masters stammerings. Brother Patrick obediently and patiently listened to and guided me throughout my scribblings. In gratitude, I dedicated the opus to him with 'An Lacha', an ode to free verse, by the Cork poet, Seán Ó Ríordáin:

Maith is eol dúin scéal na lachan
Éan nár gealladh riamh di
Leabhaireacht coisíochta;
Dúchas di bheith tuisleach
Is gluaiseacht léi ainspianta
Anonn is anall gan rithim
Is í ag marcaíocht ar a proimpe:
Ba dhóigh leat ar a misneach
Gur seo chughat an dán díreach
Nuair is léir do lucht na tuigse
Gur dícheall di vers libre.

(Well do we know the story of the duck.
A bird never blessed with loose-limbed ease.
It is natural for her to be unsteady
And her movement is outrageous.
Over and back without rhythm
Riding on her rear-end.
You would imagine from her pride
That here before you is strict metre.
But the informed know
that it's much more like *vers libre*.)

102

The academic exercise of compiling and analysing these beautiful, if little known, religious songs in Irish paved the pathway for us towards a sound recording of this repertoire. So still in that creative first year of the new decade of the 1980s, we released the first of several recordings of religious songs with the monastic community of Glenstal Abbey.

A dream come true, actually. Some months before we had ever met the monks, Mick and I were staying in Mount Marian. In the middle of the night, I sat bolt upright in the bed, still in sleep-time. 'Look at the monks, Mick,' I cried out excitedly. 'They're singing with us.' So convinced was Mick of the vision that he asked, 'How many of them?' 'Twelve,' I replied. I can still recall the dream but one little detail is amiss: the dream-time monks were processing in brown habits; Benedictines wear black!

Caoineadh na Maighdine still captures the sound of that happy, glorious year for me. We had great fun during the rehearsals and the recording was a blessed time. The 'twelve' gathered to record in the dead of the night in the church – the quietest, most reliable time to avoid the noisy airplanes taking off and landing in nearby Shannon airport. With one candle lighting on the altar, each note we sang really was a prayer. Somehow we all had an intuitive, unspoken accord that we would sing each song simply once, not interfering with multiple takes, which might wound their original purity and inviolability. I was so tuned into the objective musicology, the silent analysis of every song on paper, that it was pure joy for me to find another, much deeper expression of these songs through singing them with others.

103

Each song suddenly sprang into life through the rhythm of the words and music and we all, monks, Mick and I, felt the reverberations. So too did the listeners – from Charles Acton, published in the *Irish Times* on the feast of the Epiphany in 1981:

> There can surely be no better way to start this new decade than with an Irish record which is very lovely ... this is just the sort of Irish export that should be immensely encouraged ... there is a purity about her first notes that puts one in mind of a choirboy ... Of course, in fact hers is a woman's voice, but how exquisitely she uses it, with perfect intonation, total clarity and so as to give one a physical thrill with her line and its ornaments. All right, she is far from having the traditional nasal tone. To my way of thinking, this is not *sean-nós* itself, but in its own way a perfection of translating the tradition into international art.

When I first heard the actual recording of *Caoineadh na Maighdine*, in that year of 1980, I wrote from the ear of my heart the following which provided the sleeve notes:

> The actual performance of these songs in Glenstal Abbey has meant more to me than just making the kind of record which normally marks one's musical progress and area of interest at a particular time. Stereotyped studios, seas of microphones, time pressures and endless 'takes' had no part in this setting of religious music. The

absence of such features, which inevitably accompany the average recording, opened up the possibility of making this performance the most personalised and sincere outcry of the performer, for whom each phrase of a song is a constant confession or expression of being.

For the twelve monks who accompany me on this record, singing is a powerful medium of prayer inextricably bound up with their lifestyle. Such a background has had an indelible influence on my own singing. None of these songs will ever again exist for me as an isolated piece of music.

Woman speaks strongly through the religious songs of Ireland. She comes alive and breathes forth an antithesis: sometimes overpoweringly Christian, sometimes dramatically pagan; sometimes lulling the Child of God to sleep within her life, sometimes bitterly questioning the right of that same God to claim her child.

Braithimse go bhfuil na mothúcháin seo tar éis a rian a fhágáil ar mo dhearcadh ní amháin ar mo dhearcadh ar an amhránaíocht ach ar mo mheon féin. (Such emotions have immeasurably transformed not only my approach to singing, but also something within me which goes far deeper and defies articulation.)

~

And to the most blessed gift of all that year. We named our firstborn Eoin after John the Baptist, followed by the name Benedict, honouring the fervent prayers of many of the community for his delayed arrival. When we first took him out for a walk, an older neighbour and friend of Mother's, Miss O'Neill, peered into the pram and cooed, 'We thought, little Eoin Benedict, that you had lost your way!' We had waited so long for him and now this much welcomed stranger was about to change our whole lives. And my whole sense of hearing too.

My two ears were ever vigilant to the new miniature being among us. Even before he woke in the night, I was somehow alerted and awaited his whimper. Our home was altered forever. From now on, we had no control over the noises within, which ricocheted morning, noon and night. We could be in command of his eating habits, but we could never organise his vocal outbursts. Mick and I sang to him constantly, rhyming an alphabetical wall-hanging in the kitchen: '*A is for Apple; B is for Bear; C is for castles in the air ...* '

When Eoin was about two years old, he and I took a trip to the beautiful nature trail of Clare Glens. Mick had the car that day so off we headed on foot, taking a shortcut through the fields. Half-way across, a farmer shouted out to us, 'Watch out, I'm keeping a bull here in this next field, so don't come near the fence'. I grabbed hold of Eoin's hand and we raced the rest of the way. Safely out, I asked him, 'Eoini, were you afraid? Because I was.' 'Ah no, Mama,' he said. 'I wasn't afraid. But my tummy was!' A very early articulation of the body-brain contradiction! And a first sign of Eoin's innate natural courage and resilience.

In-Dia – The Sacred Space
of a Lifetime

S OON AFTER THE DEBUT ALBUM WITH
the monks, Mick and I were to take a life-
changing journey. Arranged by the Irish
Department of Foreign Affairs and hosted
by the Indian counterpart, the Indian Coun-
cil of Cultural Relations, we travelled to India. Even
though it was only for four weeks, it broke our hearts to
leave our two-year-old Eoin, although once we'd left
him with our good friends, the Maher family in
Murroe, he was perfectly happy to see us go. I will
never forget his happy little face at the gate as he
bravely quacked to us, 'Bye Mama, Bye Dada', wearing
his yellow Donald Duck t-shirt, a visual icon of the
sound of his voice!

The trip utterly transformed us, opening up some
profound passages in our lives. I have learned to recognise and listen to the huge role which it has played in my
life, spiritually and musically, and I have returned to
India countless times since. But this first visit was one of
the great blessings in my life of song, as I discovered
the perfect instruments I needed to refine my inner
and outer singing voice – the 'shruti' (Sanskrit for
'sacred sound') drone box, and the Indian harmonium.

We traversed this most spiritual country, lecturing, playing and singing, but also obtaining a glimpse of this exotic, gentle people.

The English word 'God' is a German version of the Greek *'Theos'*, which in turn is originally from a Sanskrit root that has also given us *'Dieu'* in French, *'Dio'* in Italian, and of course our word for the Divine in Irish, *'Dia'*. (Another wonderful little Irish word, meaning a 'diary', is *'dialann'*, literally 'the place of God'.) Our attention, whether written down, spoken out loud or silent, to everyday events is simply living in the house of God. Isn't it fascinating too that on the one hand, this Irish three-letter word, one for Creator, Christ or Spirit, meaning Absolute Good, is also the root for absolute sin and evil, *'diabhail'*. Is it possible that every sacred word contains within it the sound of its antonym?

Little wonder then that whenever I see the name of India, I cannot help but insert a hyphen – In-Dia – because 'In God' perfectly describes this country wreathed in spirituality. God has a language all of its own, from Murroe to Mumbai, and we could understand it there 'in *Dia*'. God is *uile-láithreach* (always and ever present) whether you are in Ireland or far away in India, if we opt for listening with our heart-ear.

Two blessed afternoons stand out. One was when we sensed the Indian hospitality of the Dagar brothers at their home in Calcutta. Legendary singers and leading exponents of Dhrupad singing, the source of all Indian classical music, I had a music epiphany that evening that turned my perceptions of sound back to front. Crossing the threshold into their private lives and place, we knew the privilege of seeing them off-stage. Every intimate moment with Nasir Aminuddin and Nasir Mohinuddin was a prayer.

First, Nasir Mohinuddin introduced us to the mystical Sanskrit concept of 'Nada' – the life principle or creative breath of humanity that comes from vibrations that can only be heard from within. This creative sound is God whose word precedes the visible light. Then Nasir Aminuddin invited us to sound with him the most sacred of Sanskrit syllables – Om. To chant 'Om' is to become the source and centre of the universe where the Silent One resides, he claimed. Om is the supreme mantra in the Hindu tradition; formed from three letters, 'aum', a diphthong, merges 'a' and 'u' with 'm' in a trinity which is one single sound only. This contraction of a three-letter word, which literally means 'to sound out boldly', is revered for its intrinsic power as sound, both oral and aural. It is the supreme sacred sound of the Buddhist as well as the Hindu cosmos that opens the gateway to God.

As we sang, a truth emerged that lifted the veils of otherness between us. Every religion has its own vocabulary sounds with acoustic powers. We Christians have our own cosmic sister-sound which is the 'Word'. 'In the beginning was the Word, and the Word was with God and the Word was God … And the Word became flesh and lived among us … ' (John 1:1, 14). Om/aum and the Word have been humming away since creation was formed. What strange bedlam do all of God's worshippers' voices make as they lift them up to the Lord in disparate language sounds, cadences, rhythms and timbres! The sound unites.

Quite apart from this sound interconnection, I was drawn out of my spiritual shell of complacency and

109

something profound stirred in me. As we sipped tea I felt a Divine presence, which transported me back in time and vision to the Fra Angelico painting on the wall of the Dún Lughaidh music room. That afternoon, I sensed precisely how writer and philosopher George Steiner defined this Annunciation painting as an analogy, a metaphor for an encounter with the aesthetic, the Divine, the transcendent. 'The first acquaintance is of "a terrible beauty" or gravity breaking into the small house of our cautionary being. If we have heard right the wing-beat and provocation of that visit, the house is no longer habitable in quite the same way as it was before. A mastering intrusion has shifted the light (that is very precisely non-mystically, the shift made visible in Fra Angelico's Annunciation).'[16]

16. Steiner, *Real Presences,* University of Chicago Press, 1989, p. 143.

There was another moment of fascination and charm in our Indian Summer stay when we visited Mahatma Gandhi's ashram. In preparation for the Indian advent, I was reading this Hindu pacifist's enthralling biography by journalist Louis Fischer. The biographer relates that when Mahatma read the Beatitudes, he wrote in his diaries that these golden laws 'went straight to the heart'.

The Beatitudes were close to our hearts too – the day before we packed our bags for India, Mick and I, along with the monks of Glenstal, had made a recording of these magnificent axioms. These eight universal maxims, the first sermon of Christ recounted in Matthew, Chapter 5, are the perfect ingredients for a recipe of life and truth:

Then he began to speak and taught them, saying:

'Blessed are the poor in spirit, the kingdom of heaven is theirs.

Blessed are those who mourn, they shall be consoled.

Blessed are the gentle, they shall inherit the land.

Blessed are those who hunger and thirst for justice, the justice of God shall be theirs.

Blessed are the merciful, mercy shall be shown unto them.

Blessed are the pure of heart, they shall behold their God.

Blessed are those who bring peace, they shall be children of God.

Blessed are those who suffer in the cause of right, the kingdom of heaven is theirs.'

Gandhi believed that the 'way of truth' is wholesome and keeps us sane. 'But for my faith in God, I should have been a raving maniac.' Prayer for him was 'the key of the morning and the bolt of the evening'. His prayer for humanity is moving beyond words. 'God, as truth, has been for me a treasure beyond price. May he be so for every one of us.'

At his ashram that afternoon, I experienced the power of silence midst the teeming noisiness all around us – the two theme songs of the epic sonata that is India.

111

Waiting for God

L ATER THAT YEAR OF 1982, MICK WAS on sabbatical leave from UCC and we lived for nine months at Chapel Lake Cottage in Glenstal Abbey. My abiding memory of those blissful days is of two books that watered the seeds in my soul of listening to God.

One February morning, Brother Ciarán arrived with what he called 'two of the best one hundred books that have to be read': Simone Weil's *Waiting for God* and *Finnegans Wake* by James Joyce. I was instantly drawn to the Weil book, its original French title being *Attente de Dieu* – '*attente*' being a close relation of '*attendre*', 'to listen'. Then I noticed that it was first published in the year of my nativity in 1951. So this book was first up to be read.

Simone Weil was a French writer, philosopher and mystic. She was born in Paris in 1909 into a secular Jewish family. Although strongly attracted to Catholicism, she was never baptised. She contracted tuberculosis during the Second World War, and further weakened by a series of starvation protests that was symptomatic both of a serious eating disorder and anti-Nazi demonstrations, died of cardiac arrest in 1943 at the age of thirty-four. I was caught unawares by two experiences of Weil's, which are examples of the power of the sense of hearing.

Her first revelatory experience was in the act of listening to plainchant; the second, in the act of memorisation through an aural and oral encounter with a religious poem.

On a visit to the Benedictine monastery of Solesmes, France, in 1938, she first wrote that on simply listening to the plainchant, 'each sound hurt me like a blow ... in the unimaginable beauty of the chanting and the words ... the Passion of Christ entered into my being for once and for all'.[17] This made perfect sense to me. Plainchant still bowls me over, shapes and cleanses me like rain water renewing the face of the earth.

17. Weil,
Waiting for God,
Routledge and
Keegan Paul
Ltd, 1951,
p. 20.

Weil's second aural experience was also at Solesmes, where she first read the metaphysical English poets of the seventeenth century. She particularly warmed to a poem by George Herbert called 'Love', which she learnt 'off by heart' and stored therein, where it engendered an intimate relationship with God – the essence of that little three-word phrase for memorisation.

The truth of this profound 'off by heart' experience is that it is not reliant on the visual text but on the effect of the actual verbal sounds on the body. This recitation 'by heart' and aloud was her transformation of body and spirit prayer to God. It had to do with the actual experience of reciting the prayer, becoming the prayer in sound and story. It is a powerful poem to say aloud. Try it. Let the sound of your voice soothe your spirit as you speak:

Love bade me welcome, yet my soul drew back,
Guilty of dust and sin.
But quick-ey'd Love, observing me grow slack
From my first entrance in,

113

Drew nearer to me, sweetly questioning
If I lack'd anything.

'A guest,' I answer'd, 'worthy to be here';
Love said, 'You shall be he.'
'I, the unkind, the ungrateful? Ah, my dear,
I cannot look on Thee.'
Love took my hand and smiling did reply,
'Who made the eyes but I?'

'Truth, Lord, but I have marr'd them; Let my shame
Go where it doth deserve.'
'And know you not,' says Love, 'who bore the blame?'
'My dear, then I will serve.'
'You must sit down,' says Love, 'and taste my meat.'
So I did sit and eat.[18]

18. 'Love', *The Oxford Book of English Verse: 1250–1900,* edited by Sir Arthur Quiller-Couch, Clarendon, 1919, No. 286.

Weil, a deeply spiritual visionary who waited for God in obedient, listening patience, describes the memorisation-effect which goes far beyond the superficial, the external and the obvious. 'The consequence of this practice is extraordinary and surprises me every time, for, although I experience the routine each day, it exceeds my expectation at each repetition.'[19] New, unfamiliar sound always calls forth attention but it is maintaining that freshness of occasion that Weil is hinting at here.

19. Weil, *Waiting for God,* p. 24.

Learning by heart was nothing new to her. In the Judaism that she rejected, memorising sacred texts was and still is the way to God. Committing the Torah, the

114

religious literature of the Jews, to memory is the first stage of encounter; meaning, interpretation and understanding follow. Indeed memorisation is a lost art in contemporary society.

George Steiner regrets the danger to heart knowledge: 'There is no doubt that patterns of articulate speech, reading habits ... are under pressure ... we know less by heart.'[20] Speaking, thinking, committing to memory and acting upon the heart-work is a powerful quartet of human experience that Weil knew well. Reading between the lines, what she is intimating is that the learning 'off by heart' of the sound of the sacred word was essential to being. It is a very mature practice in the age-old pursuit of wisdom and spiritual advancement.

In her openness to receive ambient, cosmic sound, in the certain kind of listening that she paid to the monastic chant around her, beauty resounded and was in the ear of the listener and continued to reside there from then on. I instinctively knew what she was trying to describe – a certain aural event that does not go away. There is a permanence that a certain type of listening promises.

Reading *Waiting for God*, a forgotten memory emerged. It harked back to my boarding-school days. We had St Luke's entire gospel, with its beautiful Mary story and song, 'off by heart' when I was in fifth year. Weil's book allowed me to revisit the pitter-patter sound of this 'Good News', which has been my strength and my song since. Of course, even when we read silently, we are verbalising internally in the ear of the heart, so it's impossible really to read without hearing. There is an inner sounding always at work.

20. Steiner, *After Babel: Aspects of Language and Translation*, Oxford University Press, 1974, p. 467.

James Joyce's awareness of the all-pervasive nature of the ear rings out from his final masterpiece, *Finnegans Wake*, Brother Ciarán's second gift to me. In all of his works, Joyce experimented with aural sounding. Joycean word-choice does not always represent the object it refers to but depends on the timbre or the characteristic sound quality of the reader's voice. His words were primarily chosen for their sound. He revered and respected all the sounds, not simply of the English language, but many others too. What he heard in his travels he wrote down. He wanted to bypass the old walls of language limitations and was wholly alive to the excitement of a marriage of multi-lingual sounds.

Ulysses, the work of Joyce's stream of consciousness, is a book of the light and the daytime, where the mind talks to itself. *Finnegans Wake*, on the other hand, is a product of the night, full of night-time activity and dream language, where Joyce speaks to the listening ear rather than the reading eye.

What is interesting is that when explaining the mysterious, nocturnal language of *Finnegans Wake*, Joyce himself advocated listening to it rather than reading it. Rational understanding is the daytime work of the eye; understanding the absurd or that which is not in accordance with reason is the full-time work of the ear and is much more productive in the night. In the dark when there are no visual distractions, the ear settles down to serious heart work. (Nicodemus, the good Pharisee of John's gospel, knew this truth.) Of the *Wake*, the author wrote in a letter to his daughter, Lucia: 'In a word, it is pleasing to the ear ... That is enough, it seems to me.'[21] According to his biographer, Richard Ellman, Joyce watched over and chose every

21. James Joyce in a letter to Lucia Joyce, 1 June 1934, quoted in Richard Ellman, *James Joyce*, Oxford University Press, 1963, p. 702.

word on its sound. Joycean scholar David Norris writes that on the completion of *Finnegans Wake*, 'to those who found it unreadable, he [Joyce] suggested not reading but listening to it'.[22] This great book of night-time activity really should be listened to in order to capture its wildness. 'The reader's Golden Rule is when in doubt, read aloud.'[23] According to Richard Ellman, Joyce 'defended its technique or form ... on the importance of sound ...'[24]

The different blessed whisperings of these two books, Weil's *Attente de Dieu* and Joyce's *Finnegans Wake*, prompted me to listen to that inner voice calling me to some day write my own aural story.

22. David Norris, *Joyce for Beginners*, Icon, 1996, p. 150.

23. Ibid., pp. 4/150.

24. Ellman, *James Joyce*, p. 703.

Enter Mícheál Patrick 'Moley' Ó Súilleabháin ... and Hildegard von Bingen

THE YEAR 1984 BROUGHT YET ANOTHER marvellous grace from God: the arrival of our second son, Mícheál Patrick, or Moley. Many evenings during my pregnancy, when I would be putting Eoini B to bed, I'd read to him from the children's classic, *The Wind in the Willows* by Kenneth Grahame. Eoin's favourite character was the first-up, gentle, homely Mole, whom he soon named 'Moley'. So Moley had to be the pet name for the new intruder of a little brother. He lived up to his literary foil since this Moleman, although overawed by the healthy chaos and hurly-burly of this new-found family trinity, adapted brilliantly and survived to tell the tale! The lads soon became firm friends and I have many, many happy memories from when they were young boys, and later indeed when singing with them as young men.

One Moley memory is from 1990 when Mick was appointed a visiting lecturer in Boston College. There was great excitement in the house the night before we left. Half-packed cases strewn in the hallway, we had to pick our steps up to bed. As usual, we knelt down at the bedside to say our night-prayer, which on this eve of departure ran something like: 'Now, lads, we're praying here for the last time for God's blessing to look after us while we are away.' Moley, just about six years old, lilted, 'Goodbye now, God. We're going to Boston tomorrow. Talk to you when we come home!' Still the same Moleman, laid-back and confident that all shall be well.

—

Psalm 139 is truly an anthem of magnificent trust and of 'just what the doctor ordered' in terms of making sense of the miracle of pregnancy: 'For it was you who formed my inward parts; you knit me together in my mother's womb, I praise you for I am fearfully and wonderfully made. Wonderful are your works …'

Pregnancy had not only stirred changes in my physical shape but had also altered my voice. For the duration of the two pregnancies, although four years apart, the one constant was that my voice wanted to sing at an even higher pitch. I welcomed this change and consciously directed that sound into the little resident in my womb. Actually, way before I discovered the astounding fact that the sense of hearing is the first sense to develop in the womb, I was acutely alive to the tiny live ear within me. At every opportunity, I tenderly sang to these little indwelling hearers. Somehow I believed that this first womb sound would form their little hearing hearts; we can infer that an expectant mother who bathes herself in the sound of God in prayer would also surround her embryonic child with those same sounds. The aural message, the messenger and the receiver are united momentarily in that sound field.

119

The other two physical feminine cycles of my life –
menstruation and menopause – also awoke this same
spirit of vocal adventure and surprise. Every monthly
menses was a time of change for me in the sound, the
timbre of my own voice. Although it alarmed me at first,
as I sang with this new voice, my fears yielded to new
acceptance. Very early on, I was aware that my voice
plummeted from almost a Coloratura, high Soprano to
a Mezzo-Soprano, lower range during this monthly
period. Then, some years ago in Boulder, Colorado, I
met an eminent voice teacher called Arthur Samuel
Joseph, who gave a possible explanation for the varying
range in voice, linking it to the physical changes that
happen in the female body every month.

Menopause in my early fifties was a few hot flushes,
but no real mood swings or nocturnal perspiring, such
as experienced by friends. Menopausal symptoms
were lessened by singing every sound in my vocal
range and exercises in deep breathing. Unknown to my
rational self, I thus created my own hormone replace-
ment treatment.

Back to around the time of Moley's birth, a twelfth-
century Benedictine Abbess, the first known female
composer in Western classical music and plainchant,
Hildegard von Bingen, entered my life. As 'a feather on
the breath of God' is how she defined her long life of
trust and promise in the Lord. I was singing at a Celtic
Spirituality conference in Dublin and the main speaker
was the controversial Californian theologian, Matthew
Fox. I was mesmerised by the sheer sound of his voice
that evening, as I was to be many times in the years that
followed when I went on the road with him in America.

I sat listening to this extraordinary orator, who used no notes whatsoever, who rather spoke 'off by heart' for over two hours.

Later as we chatted over tea, I humbly gave him a copy of my latest recording, *Good People All*. He opened out the booklet within and immediately picked up on my singing partners, the Benedictine monks of Glenstal. 'Have ye sung any of the medieval Benedictine mystic's chants – Hildegard von Bingen? I would love to hear you singing those wild melodies,' he said. 'Who?' I asked. He wrote down the name of this German medieval mystic for me and subsequently sent me on many books about her, including two which he had written himself.

The monks and I were rehearsing for an upcoming television programme, and at our next gathering I came out with this name, incredulous at the secrecy which these monks held around their Benedictine sister, one of their own. An older monk, now passed over, shook his head and said, 'Hildegard von Bingen! Oh for heaven's sake, that's eroticisation of the chant, Nóirín!' And he was right! Hildegard breaks all the rules of standard plainchant. Her chant for me was simply another dialect, another version of *sean-nós* spiritual song. They both share that wildness of improvisation and desire for ornamentation. Somewhere in the aural memory of the stones of her monastery, Disibodenberg, named after an Irish sixth-century saint, there was the faint Irish echo that she tuned into.

From then on I had to tell everyone about this trail-blazing woman, who although the earliest named composer in Western music and plainchant, is largely ignored. For instance, *The Grove Dictionary of Music and Musicians* only first mentions her in the 1980 edition, and even today there are still music dictionaries that carry no entry on her at all.

Interestingly, Bernard of Clairvaux, her contemporary, set out some chant parameters to which she paid no heed whatsoever. That same Bernard was canonised by Rome just twenty-one years after his death. He died on 20 August 1153 and was canonised on 18 January 1174. Furthermore, he was ordained Doctor of the Church in 1830. Abbess Hildegard, visionary, ecologist, cosmologist, preacher, prophet and teacher, is still not recognised as an official saint by the Roman Catholic Church and there are no glimmers of hope on the horizon.

With Hildegard's deepening presence in my life expanding, I found myself in Brussels giving a workshop. The prayer-chant of this 'Sybil of the Rhine', as she was also known, was my order of the day, although I failed to perceive that my enthusiasm was not entirely infectious! About twenty-five people were present, among them an English woman seated at the back of the room. I could tell for some time that she was agitated about something, fumbling in her bag, shifting in her chair and so on. Eventually, she raised her hand. 'Nóirín, can I tell you something about her,' she said rather coldly, in a very posh accent. '*Hildegaawd* was an obnoxious bitch!' I was taken aback, but there is a kernel of truth here. Hildegard chose her novices with snobbish disdain, accepting only the daughters of nobility. When confronted with this fact, she retorted, 'Would you put animals of different species in the one stall?' A wily response, but one that overlooks the homogeneity of humanity.

Despite this, her music went straight to my heart and soul. I first recorded Hildegard in the late 1980s and was consequently contacted by the Music Department of Notre Dame University in Indiana. Would I consider singing the title role of 'Anima' in her morality play, *Ordo Virtutum*? Though quaking at the daunting prospect, I recognised here a vocation, a calling from the Holy Spirit herself, and worked long and hard to step up to the role. Hildergard's morality play was ahead of its time, about one hundred years before the genre became popular. This entirely sung drama, in Latin, tells the tale of Anima, the soul's battle with the Devil. Eventually, the Virtues manage to dissuade her from falling for his snares.

According to Hildegard, Satan cannot and will never sing. One wonders if she was aware of the ancient proverb from her own Germany that runs: *'Wo man singt, da läst sich ruhig nieder – böse menschen kennan kiene lieder.'* Where there's singing, fear no wrong – evil people have no song. In this sung opera, Lucifer's interventions are furious, yelled screams. The young man playing this part had a voice that was bloodcurdling. He was also an extremely attractive, dark-haired fellow. So when he would approach me with his taunts, roaring into my ear, my struggle with bewitchment and being swept off my feet became all the more authentic! But night after night, the good virtues kept me on the straight and narrow. We performed this hour-and-a-quarter oratorio from Indiana to Kalamazoo. Our audiences had an English translation of the text but scarcely opened it. Instead they simply listened motionless, captivated by the otherworldly sounds of the Latin all around them.

I have relative, as opposed to perfect, pitch, which means that if I were to sing, let's say, an 'A' off the top of my head, it might not always be absolutely accurate. I might be a little left or right of centre, a little higher or lower than the 440 decibels that Western classical music has classified it. However, for years now I can pitch or sound a perfectly in-tune B flat just out of the blue. Singing in this scale is a visual and aural experience for me. I can see the outline of the song or improvisation vividly in my mind's eye. Indeed, NASA astronomers have discovered that the earth is constantly vibrating to a steady drone that they have defined as B flat – fifty-seven octaves down from the tone below Middle C on the piano. This mystical tone is one million billion times lower than the lowest sound that you can hear. So every time we sound the note B flat, we are harmonising with the ultimate, primeval cosmic music. This is the incarnate, cosmic sound of God. 'From heavenly, heavenly harmony, The universal frame began' (John Dryden).

The first experience that I had of this was one afternoon years ago when singing the one setting that has survived over eight hundred years of a Kyrie Eleison, 'Christe Eleison' by Hildegard. The image of a surge of starlings burst into my mind, soaring in formation, seamlessly harmonising with the ebb and flow of the sounds. Each inspired note seemed to cast a magic spell over the birds, but within the blink of an eye, on the last syllable, they had disappeared. Although I return to the chant almost daily, they never have, but the memory lingers. As the Chinese saying goes: 'The sound ceases, but the meaning goes on.'

124

Kyrie

Ky-ri — e * e — lei —
son. Chri-ste e — lei-
son. Ky-ri — e e —
lei — son. Ky-ri — e
e — lei-
son.

THIRD MOVEMENT
Awakening to Theosony

What You Cannot Avoid, Welcome

S EVEN YEARS OF MY LIFE, BETWEEN THE ages of thirty-five and forty-two, were dark and troubled. The deepest relationship and friendship in my life, that with Mícheál, began to crumble, and there seemed to be nothing either one of us could do to stop it falling apart. The destruction of the 'perfect Rectory couple' dawned and the emptiness had to be addressed. We did make some dreams come true and even made the miraculous happen. But now we were being torn apart. 'What you cannot avoid, welcome', is another Chinese proverb, and one of many words of wisdom that gave me great hope.

As we faced the future, Mícheál and I sometimes tearfully recited the Our Father. That prayer of prayers kept us going. In the anxious space between us, we directed this prayer to the God who had brought us together, stood between us, held our hands, kept our bothered minds clear, carried us through the grief and now 'would deliver us from evil'. Our new-found challenge was to fill our separate lives brimful with a kind of transformation and to very slowly begin to face a life apart, yet somehow together. The schoolroom of life teaches that time herself, that is, God's own time, heals and tills the painful green pastures between us. Marriage is a sacrament that despite all, even civil divorce, can survive and outlive the most appalling ravages of separation; it is a friendship that falls silent.

Out of the depths of '*scarúint na gcompánaigh*' (the Irish term, 'the parting of friends', which is also the title of a beautiful traditional tune from the Irish harping tradition), I found the incredible gift of silence. The important point is that silence is a contradiction in terms; to try to define or articulate it, one has to break it, interrupt it and surprise it. The paradox is that silence is both near and far off. As the riddle goes, 'You break it when you name it'. The beautiful, inspired words of Cardinal John Henry Newman kept me grounded and held my hands to guide me forward over these nightmarish years. 'Keep thou my feet. I do not ask to see, the distant scene, one step is enough for me.'

Our society, much less our institutional Church, has little to offer us for this optional rite of passage. Mutual love is recognised and toasted in and through the sacrament of marriage and that can never be denied. But in separation and divorce in our Roman Catholic tradition and expression, we are left stranded, with no ritual to acknowledge or 'bless' our parting just as the sacrament of marriage had celebrated our youth-filled friendship. Family and friends were constant gifts and treasures, lending listening ears through the emptiness and loneliness, and I am forever grateful to them.

Poems, the sound of them, were great consolers too, particularly one poignant song of lonesomeness by William Butler Yeats, 'When you are old'. This wist-

130

ful treasure was so prophetic and painted the exact picture of our fading relationship.

> And bending down beside the glowing bars,
> Murmur, a little sadly, how Love fled
> And paced upon the mountains overhead,
> And hid his face amid a crowd of stars.[25]

25. *Yeats's Poems*, edited by A. Norman Jeffares, Gill and Macmillan, 1989, p. 76.

One hundred and twenty syllables forming one hundred words tolled daily through the three four-line verse, like an Angelus bell reminding me to pause and pray for God's light and power. Inspired by his unrequited love for Maud Gonne and based upon a sonnet from a sixteenth century collection, *Sonnets pour Héléne* by Pierre de Ronsard, it came as a welcome stranger to me.

The Other Three of the 'John Quartet'

THERE HAS BEEN A QUARTET OF people, all male, and all coincidentally named John, who have touched and traced my listening, musical life. All four Johns, through their writings, verbally and musically, continue to inspire me towards new, long-forgotten ways of listening with the ear of the heart. They are contemporary composers, Seán Ó Riada and John Cage; poet and theologian, John O'Donohue; and John the Evanglist. You have already met 'Johnny Reidy', Seán Ó Riada.

⁓

JOHN CAGE

In 1990, I was invited to sing at a gala concert in Los Angeles to mark the seventieth birthday of my friend, the potter, poet, mystic and writer, M.C. Richards. When I realised that I was to share the stage with the avant-garde composer, John Cage, a very close friend of hers, I was like a silly teenager meeting their idol.

In the green room afterwards, he made straight for me, full of kind praise for my singing. I rattled on, as I still do, in nervous response. Two songs he was particularly touched by, he said: a plainchant rendering of the magnificent Magnificat and his all-time favourite poem of William Butler Yeats, 'Song of Wandering Aengus', which he recited then and there.

But suddenly, John's mood changed. There was a heavy silence. I translated it as a shift in his attention from me and prepared myself for him to move on. But he didn't. He seemed to be hearing another space and time, his face so transformed in an instant that I hardly recognised him. Stepping towards me as if he was about to tell me his deepest secret, this small man questioned: 'Tell me, did you know Joe Heaney at all?' Although I'd never met the man, of course I knew the singing of this extraordinary Connemara *sean-nós* singer, intimately. Taking a step backwards from this bright-eyed composer, I opened my mouth and out of the silence came a chorus of one of Joe's religious songs, '*An tAiséirí*' (The Resurrection): '*Agus aililiú lá gus aililiú ló ...*' John, eyes closed, listened intently. Tears ran down his cheeks as he talked about his friendship with this singing genius, Seosamh Ó hÉanaí, and how he had written one performance piece, 'Roaratorio' – an Irish circus based on Joyce's *Finnegans Wake* – entirely around and for his beloved Joe. Thus the read-aloud masterpiece again visited my life.

Later that evening at the banquet that followed, the finger of the Holy Spirit herself placed me at the same table as this extraordinary figure. He, being the '*fear mór*' (the big man) directed the conversation about two things over the course of the meal: mushrooms (the meal's starter that evening, and John being, as he humbly informed us, a world authority on the subject); and the whole realm of silence, which was his primary preoccupation.

133

I timidly told him about the effect that '4.33' had on me back in university in 1968. John explained to us that he had written it as an experiment, following a Zen spiritual experience where he entered into a totally sound-proofed, six-walled studio to discover what physical silence might be. Two sounds almost deafened him – a high-pitched sound which he later learned was his own nervous system, and a low-pitched sound, his blood circulation. But '4.33' was no random, chaotic composition – it was carefully born and sculpted 'in proportional notation', he called it; that is, the score consisted of five blank pages, except for a long dividing line down the page which indicated a time span of fifty-six seconds.

That night, back in the silence of my hotel room, full of inspiration, I began to put flesh on the bare bones of a book that I would later publish. I was forty, going through the raw and empty days of a relationship breakdown and finding it a huge time of change. Actually, I carried in my bag a book containing the inspired, encouraging words of Carl Jung: 'All true things must change and only that which changes remains true.'

A month or so later, back home in the quotidian role of motherhood once again, the phone rang: 'This is John Cage. Do you remember me?' Sure, I hadn't stopped boasting about our meeting since! The call was to invite me to sing the part of Seosamh Ó hÉanaí in 'Roaratorio' at the prestigious contemporary music festival in Huddersfield. There, one afternoon, during a tea-break from rehearsal, I told John of how he had inspired me greatly in so many ways and that I would be celebrating that inspiration with my little book of forty chants for forty years. 'The skeleton is nearly fleshed out,' I told him. 'Chants to sing – chance to pray.' He listened fixedly and I was at that very moment so aware of his outstanding instinct for listening with the heart-ear. There and then, he offered to publicly endorse the work. I screamed so excitedly that the entire cast rushed over to hear what merited such an ungodly response – all worried that, in the effort, I would have strained my voice and that evening's show would have to be cancelled! I never sang better.

During the Huddersfield festival, we did a television interview with audience participation. John taught me a lot about how to handle the media that day. At one point, a spiky question was put to him about his music. I cannot remember the gist of the interrogation but we watched and waited for him to reply. After a period of inappropriate silence, which he was a veteran at staging, he simply said in his high-pitched, rather strangulated voice, 'Now that's not a very interesting question, let's move on to the next'!

There is another story about John's way with words, which Abbot Patrick Hederman told me one evening. A friend of John's was inflexibly insistent that he should accompany her to a performance of Handel's 'Messiah'. He had absolutely no interest in the oratorio, but his so-called friend persisted, went ahead and bought the tickets, forcing him into acceptance. Over the applause, she screamed at him: 'Now, John, aren't you delighted you came? Aren't you so moved by it?' He retorted: 'I don't mind being moved, but I sure hate being shoved!'

Alas the endorsement of my little chant book was never to be because John sadly died some months later. And yet, there are moments when he endorses my singing and my life from beyond. I await the next. (*Gregorian Chant Experience* was published by the O'Brien Press and would never have come into existence were it not for the meticulous editing and wonderful support of Íde Ní Laoghaire, daughter of my original mentor, Pilib.)

—

JOHN O'DONOHUE

I first met John O'Donohue on the evening of 2 October, the Feast of the Guardian Angels, 1997, in the garish lobby of the Intercontinental Hotel in New York. I was about to start a tour of the States with him to launch his bestselling first book, *Anam Chara*.

We naturally greeted one another in Irish. His '*Dia dhuit, a chroí*' (God be with you, oh one of my heart) was met by my '*Dia is Muire dhuit freisin*' (God and Mary be with you too). Miraculously, and in that moment, we had found, guided by the Guardian Angels, a common, safe, sound language. Both of us had come to value the sheer magic of that language, the second-oldest organised sound in Europe, in our early twenties. On that trip and in the following years, Irish was to be our first language, our own morse code, whenever we were alone or amid strangers.

For two of the happiest weeks of my life, I accompanied this gentle giant, with the booming sonic laugh, from Boston to Sante Fé up to Seattle – where his *anam bhráthair* (brother friend), poet David Whyte, joined us on stage on our 'Celtic Wisdom' tour of America. In bookshops, churches, on TV and radio, John would read from his book and I did my best to respond to the beauty of his eloquent writings in song. As we traversed that vast country, every space was alive

136

and vibrant for him. Every landscape, every horizon was the 'First Scripture', as he called it.

Our first 'duet' was in an Anglican church in New York. John was clad in a dark green jacket, dark grey shirt and red tie. He loved the colour red – the 'hue of the climate of existence', he called it. 'In the beginning the Word was *red* ... And the wound in the unseen Spilled forth the red weather of being', enlivening John's body and soul.[26]

26. O'Donohue, 'In Praise of Fire', *Benedictus*, Bantam Press, 2007, p. 30.

We sat tensely on a chaise longue, the only seating area in the sacristy. He broke the silence: 'Anyway, the important thing here, Nór, is that we "mind" one another.' And that was the concise first commandment of the entire time. We did mind and take care of one another.

One evening in Boulder, Colorado, I returned to our quaint hotel, the Boulderado, to join John for supper. 'You missed it today, Nór, *a chroí*. I had such unique intimacy with a group of about twenty oul mystics. We just sat there in the silence together, deciphering our destinies and just being ourselves. You'd have loved it, Nór.' He seemed as genuinely disappointed as I that I had missed this experience, and he waxed flamboyantly on and on about it in Irish. As I probed and queried about who these twenty great sages were and where they came from, he dissolved into one of his hilarious, uncontrolled laughs. The mystics were some mountain goats that he had come upon in a field as he walked out of town. He sat down among them just gazing at them for at least two hours. No person can experience silence in a way an animal does or in a way that a landscape can, he would often observe. John, who was reading some Christmas sermons of Meister Eckhart

137

at the time, was fond of quoting him: 'Nothing resembles God as much as silence' and 'There is a place in the soul of pure tranquillity'.

John's poetry collection, *Conamara Blues*, was waiting to be born from the soul-womb during those days. His wonderful cycle of Rosary sonnets began to form in Santa Fé. 'Now, don't tell anyone that I'm writing this oul cycle,' he whispered to me one brunch time, 'it's a very good idea, you know, and someone might steal it on me!' I shared with him my passion for the Rosary, the full twenty decades, which is a daily prayer-stop for me. (Just on that point, I think that one of the most inspired moves of Pope John Paul II was to augment the traditional Rosary with five more decades to amplify and complete the life history of Christ.)

I remember him talking beautifully about his desire to write the definitive biography of Jesus. 'There are a lot of writers trying to capture the Christ out there, but they just don't bring the bacon in from the gate. I mean, what were his dreams made of? What made him weep? His beautiful hands. His *uaisleacht anama* (nobility of soul).' *Conamara Blues* was published a year later; the Christ story remained an unfinished dream for him, now waiting to be truly told.

It was the capacity of John's own *uaisleacht anama* that tempted me to share my secret soul desire with him, which was to undertake a doctorate on the sound of God. His warmth and blessing of this scary undertaking was more than enough to guide my next step. As truthful as I could be, I stammered, like Moses, about my own life-long experience of that sound. 'When we are true to ourselves, we are true to God,' he often said to me. 'I want to see everything you write on this. You

138

are on a new horizon of beginning.' He went on further to give me some personal advice which I wrote down there and then, and it proved to be three sentences that changed my life. 'Always give yourself the opportunity of silence, Nór,' he said. 'Every single sound has silence beside, behind, before and within it. Begin now to develop what I sense is your unique listening blessing in order to hear the silent song of your own wild spirit.'

Another morning, on a car journey to Seattle, I was in the back contemplating aloud my thoughts and my fears of beginning the theological journey. Suddenly he reached into his bag and took out the book that he had been reading: a collection of letters by Boris Pasternak, the Russian twentieth-century poet and writer. He admired this man tremendously for his heart-novel, *Doctor Zhivago*. John had the perfect Pasternakian quote for me, which he later wrote down in my diary: 'When a great moment knocks on the door of your life, its sound is often no louder than the beating of your heart and it is very easy to miss it.' This was the final prompting I needed to embark on this daunting, yet crucial study.

The capital of the state of New Mexico, Santa Fé, which is Spanish for 'Holy Faith', holds a blessed, holy faith moment for me, forming another thread in the emerging tapestry of a theology of listening. This town of sacred belief is very proud of welcoming the stranger, as it did with the wonderful artist Georgia O'Keeffe, who lived there for some years before she passed over in 1986. They had just opened a museum dedicated to her works. John was a genius at the visual as well as the verbal so we had to visit it. Once in, we went our separate ways. But at some stage, I stumbled

on John beholding a painting from her series 'Blue and
Green Music'. Programme notes convinced us that it
was her interpretation of music in colour. We read how
she once remarked that 'singing has always seemed to
me the most perfect means of expression. It is so spon-
taneous … Since I cannot sing, I paint'.

He stood with his arms outstretched in rapture, awe
and admiration. Visually illiterate myself, I have never
been so moved by anyone's becoming totally one with
the object of perception. He was transfigured. For that
moment it was his entire world. Later, I sensitively
referred to that moment and in the course of the conversation he made a personal comment to me which
gave me further confidence to engage with research on
Divine listening, hearing and silence. 'You could
express how the aural meets the visual in listening to
God in the same way that O'Keeffe expresses how the
visual encounters the aural.' He promised to be an ally,
and he was.

It took a few years, but as the chapters of the doctorate on an aural theology evolved, I passed some first
drafts before him. He was a difficult task-master. I was
resisting a theological language, which I deemed to be
hijacked by clerical, male-dominated, stilted, convo-
luted and intellectual voices. 'But theology has every
right to be so,' he insisted. 'If you are to become a doctor in theology, you have to learn and write in that language.' And he was right. I had to start again.

The last conversation I had with him was some
months before his death, over the telephone, when
he, as he always did in every conversation, told me a
funny story. Strangely this one had to do with the
heaven that called him back too soon. He rang me

one morning en route to America. 'Now I've a great story, *Dochtúir Ní Riain*. I thought of you immediately with your two aunts, the nuns, when I heard it! An elderly sister dies, meets Peter at the oul pearly gates, and says to him, "Now, I've loved God and Jesus and the Holy Spirit and all that. But, all my life, I've been waiting to meet Mary." "Go on, there she is, standing over there by the wall," Peter replied. So the sister makes her way over to Mary. "Oh Mary. I've literally been dying to meet you. Now God, the Son and Holy Spirit are grand, but you've always been the one for me! I just have one question for you. Why is it that down on earth, all your pictures and statues are all so dolorous and sad?" "Well, you see," whispered Mary, beckoning her to the corner, "I was always hoping that t'would be a girl!"' Then he roared down the phone with laughter. Although I often thought about him over those few months before he passed over, I never lifted the phone to talk to him, thinking that he would be here for an awful lot longer. It is a lesson: do not postpone a gesture to a treasured one.

John left this life on 4 January 2008, just three days after his fifty-third birthday. On three dream-time occasions, he has visited me. The trio of dreams were filled with light and laughter. In the most recent one, he called me into a book-filled room, reassuring me that he would continue to mind me at all costs. 'I love it how since I passed over, there isn't a single day that you're not talking about me, reading my oul books for people, and sure, when I was alive, you never mentioned me at all at all.' It's true! By the glint in his eye, I knew through the dream that he was at rest. His lifelong quest for eternal beauty and belonging was finally at an end.

It was an honour to sing at his funeral Mass in St Patrick's Church, Fanore, Co. Clare, on the bleak, rainy morning of 12 January 2008. Even nature's elements were weeping for Dr O'Donohue that morning. It was clear to me what John would have wanted to hear from me: the Beatitudes, those eight principles of the religion that he was totally committed to and the very first sermon of the person of his desired biography. 'Blessed are those who mourn, they shall be consoled.'

―

JOHN THE EVANGELIST

Of all four Johns, John the Evangelist, in his clairaudient Gospel, taught me the most about listening. He has been a word-to-ear friend for years, shaping my hearing even from his very first words: 'In the beginning was the Word ...' (At the age of fifteen in Dún Lughaidh, I had loved the enforced practice of learning this beautiful scripture (along with Luke's) 'off by heart'.)

The hidden treasure in John's gospel for me is three-fold and spirals upwards: from the finite, cosmic sound of nature, such as the wind, through the finite sound of the voice of Jesus Christ, up to the infinite silent Voice of God. This dramatic gospel lends itself to a reading, a listening and an interpretation which is far more than an historical story. This is truly inspired – from Latin *'inspirare'*, which means 'to breath into'. The unique turn of phrase of John's Christ immediately draws us in. The important lesson one feels, on reading this poetic, dramatic work, is the power of the gospel as God's self-revelation in a Word: God's Word is spoken loudly and clearly on earth through the name

142

of Christ. Listen closely to the words, take heed and yield to the message is the theme.

John paints the entire horizon of creation out of this Word. In the space between the letters, the ear and the eye assemble in pure praise; the concerto of sound chances on the canvas of light, rejoicing in the human expression of Divine revelation. 'Then God said' the creation words (Genesis 1:3), but no one listened until the 'Logos' became flesh. Put another way, humanity really only half listened; it was defective hearing until the Jesus of Wisdom appeared. What makes this Word expressive? Of course it is beyond the onomatopoeic; that is, no human word can imitate or echo the Word of God. And it is beyond the context and history of attachment which is Christianity.

The Good News according to John is particularly inclusive of the feminine on three counts. First, Christ is the embodiment of the 'logos', that ancient feminine wisdom. (In the principle Western source languages of Hebrew, Greek and Latin, the word for 'wisdom' is, usually, feminine.)

Second, John's recount of the Resurrection story centres on one woman's need for and conversion to faith; a revolution which is purely aural. Mary Magdalen's intimate conversation with Jesus appears to follow no definite agenda, plan or structure; they are both being perfectly true to the situation. The mysterious truth is this: if we encounter God and play our loving role by ear, we consent to the emotional workings of the Spirit who always promises accuracy.

Third, the noblest profession of belief in all of the New Testament is related in the John story. It is uttered by a woman – Martha. This sister of Lazarus

143

and Mary of Bethany declared to Jesus, 'Yes, Lord, I believe that you are the Messiah, the Son of God, the one coming into the world' (John 11:27). One affirmative cry, 'yes', is not sufficient to convey the depth of her belief. Jesus is the Messiah, the fulfilment of all scriptures' promises. He is the Son of God, human and divine. He is the one coming into the world, the one yet to come in glory. These three Trinitarian titles spoken and heard summarise the pinnacle of all Christian thought, male and female. But one particular verse persuasively shepherded me towards a partiality for John and it is this:

> The wind blows where it chooses, and you hear the sound of it, but you do not know where it comes from or where it goes. So it is with everyone who is born of the Spirit. (John 3:8)

I have, in the words of John himself, kept the good wine until now (John 2:10). John's gospel is a delight here in the third chapter because of the language he uses. Even in translation from the Greek, it is poetic and rhythmic human speech at its very best, signifying the essence of the sacred. In its difference, this vocabulary actually sounds strangely familiar. A half-dozen one-syllable words – 'you hear the sound of it' – sum up my ultimate liking for John's inspired description of the elusive, noisy Spirit. So it is possible to hear the sound of God! Jesus himself has left us the key with which to unlock the door of possibility and discovery. And it is this. The Spirit – which in both Greek and Hebrew is the same word for breath and wind – blows to be heard in the present, not in the past nor in the future.

144

This passage, this message, opened so many doors to the mansion of a theology of listening. It is the Spirit that initiates, nurtures and sustains a conversation between scripture and reader. It is not automatic, nor a given, for the reader. In fact, the harder the task of interpretation, the more attentive and active the Spirit. The power of the Spirit comes alive through its graced sound, 'which is present and does transform all those willing to listen'.[27] Here is an incarnation of the Spirit where spirit meets flesh through the flesh of the ear. It is Jesus telling humanity once again how to pray.

It is the Spirit in sound and not in the silent visual word that gives life. The Spirit of God is know-how and experience. Like the wind, its source and destination are unknown; like the wind and breath, it sounds and can be listened to. Belief in the spirit may lack understanding of its workings, but belief is guaranteed aurally. The source and destiny of the wind is vague and hidden. The reality, the fact, the presence of this spirit is its *sound*, which is immediately aural.

So what is the context of this aural truth which Jesus promises will make us free? It arises out of a very important conversation, indeed the first deep dialogue involving Jesus that is recalled in this gospel story.

A leader of the Pharisees, a sect totally opposed to Jesus Christ, visits him one night. The essence of their conversation is that in order to be 'reborn' into and enter the Kingdom of God, one must hear the sound of the Spirit/Wind that blows the *metanoia*, the conversion required for such an entry. Jesus was hinting at the aural, free-spirited wind.

I always wondered why Nicodemus visits Jesus at night. Some commentators say that it indicates that he

27. David
Tracy, *The
Analogical
Imagination*,
Crossroad
Publishing,
1998, p. 43.

was a shady character, but I think that is missing the point entirely. What is important here is the biological fact that even in the darkness, the vocal message or communication is orally and aurally unimpaired. Night-time is the time of hearing and listening – and the sonic wind is another melody of nightfall which I love to sing about...

> *Many's the night, love, when you lay sleeping.*
> *Dreaming of some sweet repose.*
> *While I a young girl left broken-hearted,*
> *listening to the winds that blow.*

(I learned this song from the traditional sister singers, Sarah and Rita Keane, of Caherlistrane, Co. Galway. It tells of how 'when love hid his face amid a crowd of stars', the ache is healed in and through night-air listening.)

The noisy wind is the supreme *symbol* of the Holy Spirit. Once this Spirit is heard, it brands the listener with a name on a white stone, which is the secret pin number that releases true identity. 'Let anyone who has an ear listen to what the Spirit is saying ... To everyone who conquers I will give ... a white stone, and on the white stone is written a new name that no one knows except the one who receives it' (Revelation 2:17). The sonic wind and the naming stone suggest a theology of nature as sound. The Creator is the primal music that co-relates in every sound and in the name of every living thing.

Only God hears the actual timbre of every human voice. The God of Creation is a listening God. There is a secret sonic quality in every voice and there is another hidden name for every human being that is

146

auditory and that God alone knows. God is sound, in every meaning of the word, for each one of us: the real world is the one that has its beginning in the promising sound of God.

'And Wisdom is a butterfly'
– Distant Music

O N 16 DECEMBER 1996, THE ACADEMY Award-winning actress, Anjelica Huston, orchestrated an evening of Irish poetry, prose and song at the Mark Taper Forum in Los Angeles in order to raise awareness for two United States-based organisations – Project Children and Amnesty International. Some months before, the co-creator of the evening, Michael Fitzgerald (a past pupil of Glenstal Abbey), had given her a copy of one of my recordings, *Vox de Nube*. In a glossy New York magazine that December, she nominated it as her favourite CD. I was invited to perform, to weave song in and out of the evening a half dozen times while she, her godfather Gregory Peck, and the actors Gabriel Byrne and Fionnuala Flannagan did their beautiful presentations. Blessings were abundant during those two days in Los Angeles with Anjelica and many lessons around listening with the ear of the heart were extravagantly and eloquently taught. There were two in particular that remain: one was concerned with a purring cat; the other with the elusive, chrysalis power of the spoken word to reduce the speaker and listener to tears. A line from a William Butler Yeats poem, 'Tom

O'Roughley', defined the evening: 'And Wisdom is a butterfly ...'

Michael Fitzgerald collected me at the airport and announced that Anjelica had invited us to dinner at her home in downtown Venice along with her husband, the Mexican sculptor, Robert Graham. Wild with excitement, I was also aware of the incongruity of it all, because here was I, wearing this gaudy snow-white synthetic fur jacket that I had bought earlier that day in a sale in a New York store, just about to meet a one-time model and now acclaimed actress in her extraordinary abode. But it was a glorious evening, full of fun, light and pure energy. Out of the car and up to the front door, which was set into a huge wall that hid the façade of their breathtaking house – designed by the very handsome Robert and adorned with many of his stunning human figure scuptures. I had no idea then that he was one of America's most acclaimed and respected artists. And I had yet to meet this celebrity who was in the kitchen cooking our pizza supper! But we were instantly soul-sisters, even down to our birth dates; I made my appearance in this world precisely one month before Anjelica.

Supper over, there was the next privilege of that dreamy evening. Robert Graham brought us into his studio, and we stood in awe of these beautiful human masterpieces. That Zen story of the sculptor knowing the presence of the lion hidden deep in the marble came back with powerful resonance as I gazed on, touched, even smelled the artistry all around me, heightened of course by the surreal experience of actually standing beside this inspired sculptor. I could not silence the song in my heart, and burst forth with the greatest song of salvation from the Christian tradition, 'The Magnificat Cum Alleluia'. I sang, blown away by the yearning which his imagination had created within me. The resident cats looked on in surprise!

We returned to the house, and later, as I was helping Anjelica serve coffee in her bohemian kitchen, our conversation naturally turned to these wonderful feline friends of hers who briefly came to vet this stranger. Not particularly a cat lover before this, I was touched by her sensitive, tactile relationship with them, and as she spoke to them in turn, they responded with non-stop purring. 'They purr not only as a means of communication,' Anjelica told me. 'It's also a form of self-healing, you know.' Apparently, through the constant sound vibrations of these vocal muscles rapidly tremoring, endorphins are released in the brain, which heals ailing bones and muscles and improves declining bone density. Leonardo da Vinci referred to the cat as 'nature's masterpieces'. Yes, they certainly possess the masterly skills of knowing that it is the sound that heals. (Cats have a natural sound instinct! Marmion, the monastery cat here in Glenstal, arrives precisely at 1.30 p.m. daily, scratches gently at my door, and once inside, rents my space by 'purring' for his supper until Vespers at 6 p.m.)

The following day, the day of the concert, brought its own angelic magic. A sound rehearsal was scheduled for 1 p.m. on the stage of this downtown Los Angeles theatre, with a full dress rehearsal around four. This level of meticulous preparation was strange to me and I longed for the freedom, the playing it by ear, that my own performances breathe by. But this was a theatrical production with no room for improv-

150

isation. So the timing of the songs and exact position on stage was defined well in advance and any deviation would throw the entire evening out of kilter. I would not make a good actor!

After my rehearsal I was shown to my dressing room to await the call for the complete run through. I glanced down through the programme, and was amazed to see that Anjelica's two choices were an excerpt from 'The Dead', the final short story of James Joyce's *Dubliners*, plus that Yeats poem that meant so much to me then, 'When you are old'.

I had known 'The Dead' for years, more so once I became aware of the author's direction that the sound of the words he employed to tell his tales was crucial. It is full of sonic moments, all about songs and listening. Of course, the author was a celebrated tenor and won a bronze medal for singing at Dublin's Feis Ceoil in 1904. So descriptions of voices are the unifying idea: 'Her voice, strong and clear in tone. To follow the voice ... was to feel and share the excitement of swift and secure flight ... Freddy Malins, who had listened with his head perched sideways to hear her better ... A murmur in the room attracted his attention ...'

There is one early-on narrative in 'The Dead' that resonated so loudly with my own listening story as a little girl on the shadowy steps of the stairs back in Mount Marian. What is a child sitting on the stairs in the shadow, listening to distant music, a symbol *of*?

Gretta, the wife of Gabriel Conroy, is standing near the top of the dark staircase listening to a famous singer singing 'The Lass of Aughrim' in the distance, which plucks the strings of a memory. Her husband looks on intently. 'Gabriel was surprised at her stillness

151

NÓIRÍN
NÍ RIAIN

and strained his ear to listen also ... There was grace and mystery in her attitude as if she were a symbol of something. He asked himself what is a woman standing on the stairs in the shadow, listening to distant music, a symbol *of*. If he were a painter he would paint her in that attitude ... *Distant music* he would call the picture ...'[28] Gretta is the ultimate literary symbol of listening with the ear of the heart.

28. James Joyce,
'The Dead',
Dubliners,
edited by
Robert Scholes
and A. Walton
Litz, Penguin,
1976, p. 211.

The annual Christmas gathering, and all the signs are that it is on 6 January, the feast of the Epiphany, hosted by Gabriel's two aunts, is secondary to the storyline. His wife, Gretta, is listening with the ear of the heart to the famous tenor singing, and in the very space between the listening, she herself has an epiphanic moment. She can now share, for the first time ever, her story of stories, introducing her husband to the long dead first, perhaps only, love of her life. A young singer, Michael Furey, won her heart through the sound of his voice: 'He had a very good voice, poor Michael Furey ... I think he died for me.' After her confession, she sobs her heart out and into a place of deepest sleep.

But Gabriel's sudden glimpse of personal insight and knowledge always moved me because it all has to do with the ear, listening and memory. The moral of this story is two-fold: that memory and the ear are close co-workers in the assembly line of life – one will assist the other to wholeness; and the secret of passing boldly over in glory and passion into the next world of the dead is about listening to the silent, distant snowy sound. 'His soul swooned slowly as he heard the snow falling faintly through the universe and faintly falling, like the descent of their last end, upon all the living and the dead.'[29]

29. Ibid.

Back to that Hollywood manifestation of another greatness altogether for me. For the first time, the cliché of someone 'stealing the show' made perfect sense: Anjelica was the thief of the day and night, both in rehearsal and in the moment. She embodied there and then the person of Gretta. She cried her eyes out, both at rehearsal and during the live performance. The few of us listeners in that darkened auditorium during the rehearsal did so too. This was a life-lesson for me that has lingered: there is no such event as a dress rehearsal in life. God is always listening for the true, real heart of the character.

The Magic of Seven

WHEN I EMBARKED ON THIS *auro*-biography, to let my thoughts wander where they had never entered before, I discovered that my life unfolded in a hidden time structure: every seven years a new spiritual time opened out and some experience of fullness and completion was revealed. Seven years seems to be the perfect gestation period for us to let go of what must pass and to welcome new opportunities and dreams.

In harmony with this realisation was the discovery that scripture is drenched in the number seven. Seven symbolises perfection, fulfilment, peace and accomplishment. God was exhausted after six days spent speaking into existence all of creation; on the seventh, the Creator stood in silence at the majesty and awe of the universe and all its inhabitants which came into being through the voice's sonic power. 'So God blessed the seventh day and hallowed it, because, on it, God rested from all the work that he had done in creation' (Genesis 2:3).

Then just today, 1 August 2009, at Mass here in Glenstal, the first reading is that wonderful passage where the Lord speaks to Moses on Mount Sinai, from

Leviticus, the third book of the Torah. (Actually, the
original Hebrew name of this sixth century BC third
book of the Torah and Jewish Scripture meant 'And
He called'. Three centuries later, when it was translated
into Greek, it lost its auditory title and was named
Leviticus, with very masculine connotations meaning
'the priests of the tribe of Levi'.) The Lord God
declares to Moses that any sabbatical year, any year of
Jubilee, must be measured in sevens. 'But in the seventh year there shall be a Sabbath of complete rest ...'
When all this reckoning in sevens is complete, the
God of Mount Sinai decrees that the work be cele-
brated with a trumpet blast; whatsmore, a loud one:
'Then you shall have the trumpet sounded loud'
(Leviticus 25:9).

Christ inherits and embraces the symbolism of
seven. The Gospel of John, my literary landmark, has
Jesus transform the ordinary into the extraordinary
through seven miracles. The Christ of Matthew's story
has the most important, sharp, urgent statement ever
issued to us about togetherness and love. In chapter
18, there are two inevitable revelations: 'Amen, truly I
tell you, if two of you agree on earth about anything
you ask, it will be done for you by my Father in heaven.
For where two or three are gathered in my name, I am
there among them.' Then he goes on directly to say
that the only way to shape our lives now is through
forgiveness, not to opt out in bitterness and misery. Let
it go. The power is in the hearing when it directs advice
for life. 'Then Peter said to him, "Lord, if another ...
sins against me, how often should I forgive? As many
as seven times?" Jesus said to him. "Not seven times,
but, I tell you, seventy-seven times."' The cycle of seven

NÓIRÍN
NÍ RIAIN
brings into our lives un-chosen, unknown enterprises of divine realisations that will carry us through the world and beyond.

In aurem interiorem – The Inner Ear Takes That Voice to Heart

SOMETIMES IT HAPPENS THAT WE COME across an article or a book that deliberately but subtly encourages us to climb new horizons. Two such blessings surprised me and adjusted my principles from then on: one was an article by the Benedictine Dom Sebastian Moore, and the other, a book by Bishop Joseph Duffy on St Patrick.

'All theology has to be autobiographical,' Dom Sebastian Moore claimed, a phrase that was hugely affirming for me in telling my own story. Furthermore, Moore goes on to say that there's nothing new or radical about this statement. What about one of the first and finest theological texts ever, Augustine's *Confessions*, which is an autobiography?

I was off to the library to get my hands on this book. But when I got there, I found out that it is not one book – there are no less than thirteen books of the *Confessions*! Augustine knew the business of the ear, physiologically, psychologically and theologically. The underlying message of this literary baker's dozen is one of desire for right listening. The *Confessions* are true stories, told and retold. Initially, Augustine kept many a friend in thrall by telling tales of his insightful exploits. Then he felt obliged to submit such escapades to writing – either by himself or through telling the ear of a scribe. But the stories, as in the case of Scripture, came first. The oral/aural gave way to the silent/visual. Augustine's autobiographical *Confessions* were, in origin, his admission of the truth of his life, and were heard long before they were read.

The *Confessions* are in the form of a conversation. The reader, from the outset, is a fly on the wall in the chat-space between Augustine and his God, whose power and wisdom know no boundaries. But yet, the reader is forcefully drawn in, cheering Augustine on. He eloquently and perfectly articulates, on humanity's behalf, the sum total of all Christian theology, namely that '*fecisti nos ad te et inquietum est cor nostrum, donc requiescat in te*' (you have made us for yourself, and our heart is restless until it rests in you) (*Confessions* 1:1:1). The reader of this classic line is left in no doubt that it is God who hears our longing prayer.

I became the eavesdropper in Augustine's speech to and with God and came away convinced that God is responding in the real ear of our minds. Were Augustine never to have alluded to the inner ear at all in the *Confessions*, there are signs everywhere that point to the stern reality of the aural: these are human words, divinely inspired, in praise of God.

You cannot but conclude that Augustine was aware of the biology of the ear as well as its innate possibility for banter with the Divine. But listening to the Word made flesh is bypassing the biological ear in favour of the heart. 'Everyone who belongs to the truth listens to

158

my voice' (John 18:37). In Augustine's commentary on this verse, only three things matter: listening, obeying and believing. 'He listens, of course, with the inner ear, that is, he listens to my voice, and this would mean just the same as if he were to say, "believe me".'[30]

The ear of the heart is perfectly tuned to the heart of heaven; it has a direct line to the joyful, soundful festivities of 'the house of God' Augustine promises, provided cosmic noise does not drown it out. Surely, the saint is remembering the great Christ parable of the Sower (Luke 8): the seed scattered among the thorns are the ones deafened and distracted by the cacophonous, ear-splitting sounds of the world around. They will never survive. But the good sound seeds are those that land on their feet on good soil, first and foremost listening to the good word, the good news, taking it to the heart and obediently acting justly with God, oneself and the world. A 'certain sweet and melodious strain strikes on the ears of the heart, provided only the world does not drown the sounds'.[31] We must pursue the sound field and walk therein, even though the ultimate prognosis is bleak as we hear the sounds of the groaning of human frailty. However, if we walk 'for a brief while ... within reach of that sound ... we may catch something from that house of God', Augustine promises us.[32]

Every single person's story of their relationship with the Divine is autobiography, not theology. I love Augustine's autobiography (or *auro*-biography) of his own conversion, which in the midst of psychological turmoil was auditory. God called Augustine one day in late summer or early autumn of 386 in a Milanese garden through a voice that he could only describe

30. *The Fathers of the Church, St Augustine Tractates on the Gospel of John*, translated by John W. Rettig, The Catholic University of America, 1996, Vol. 90, p. 24.

31. John Henry Parker, *Exposition on the Book of Psalms by St Augustine, Bishop of Hippo*, 1847, Vol. 2, p. 189.

32. Rettig, *The Fathers of the Church*, pp. 189, 190.

analogically: a 'voice like that of a boy or a girl, I know not which.'[33] This incessant mantra, '*tolle lege, tolle lege*'[34] – take read, take read – was truly the voice of God. This was the real calling that knew no frontiers. From the moment Augustine read aloud the true story of God's incarnate word, that story became the story of Augustine's true self. As the sound of the Word of the Lord Jesus Christ resonated through him, the ego is silenced and spiritual change to goodness vibrates. Augustine's conversion story, like St Paul's before him and his Irish counterpart, Patrick, is through the ear.

Augustine was an orator par excellence. From my debating experience in secondary school, I gazed appreciatively on this gift of his. At the age of eighteen he mastered the art of rhetoric, learning to speak eloquently and to recognise the sound of your own voice ringing in your ear. The spoken word is wisdom and its intention is to affect the thought and conduct of all who listened. It is not necessarily a question of what was being said, but how it was vocalised and sounded. Augustine didn't pick up this grace 'from the sky' – '*ní ón spéir a fuair sé é*', as we say in Irish; Ambrose, who baptised him, taught him all he knew on this level. Describing the influence of the 'sweetness of discourse' of St Ambrose, Augustine admits that he 'was not anxious to learn what he said, but merely to *hear* how he said it'.[35]

So the sound of the spoken word takes precedence over the meaning of what is being said. The heart is opened wide by the honeyed sound. In that awakening, truth is revealed. 'When I opened up my heart to receive the eloquence with which he spoke, there likewise entered … the truths that he spoke.'[36]

33. *The Confessions of Saint Augustine*, translated by John K. Ryan, Doubleday, 1960, p. 202.

34. *The Confessions of Augustine*, edited by John Gibb and William Montgomery, Cambridge University Press, 1908, viii, p. 230.

35. Ryan, *Confessions*, p. 130; italics mine.

36. Ibid., p. 131.

160

Bis orat qui cantat – the one who sings prays twice. *Bis orat qui audit* – the one who listens (with the ear of the heart) prays twice. With Indian harmonium.

FIRST THREE RECORDINGS.
Óró Damhnaigh, 1977, with the
band, L–R: Mícheál Ó Súilleabháin,
John Dwyer, Tomás Ó Catháin,
Matt Fahy and Tommy Kearney
(top). *Seinn Aililiú*, 1978 (middle).
Caoineadh na Maighdine, 1980
(right).

THE BENEDICTINE EXPERIENCE. Thirteen monks and a woman outside the monastic castle in 1981, with Abbot Augustine O'Sullivan, seventh from the left (top). Me, in white, as 'Anima' in Hildegard's liturgical drama, *Ordo Virtutum*, University of Notre Dame, Indiana, reducing the devil, in black, reluctantly and with a little help from my Virtuous friends to chains (above)!

With Brother (now Abbot) Patrick Hederman in Honan
Church, UCC, during our recording of *Vox de Nube*, Feast of
St Ciarán, 1989.

A BRUSH WITH HOLLYWOOD. Anjelica Huston (top). On the set of *Agnes Brown,* the film she directed and acted in; I sing a snippet of the 'Magnificat cum Alleluia' on screen (above).

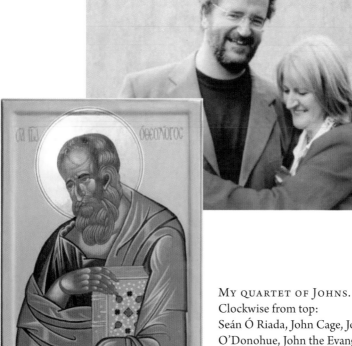

MY QUARTET OF JOHNS.
Clockwise from top:
Seán Ó Riada, John Cage, John
O'Donohue, John the Evangelist
(an icon by Fearghal
O'Farrell).

LOVELY FAMILY MOMENTS. In Cork, 1985 (top). Moley
and Eoin at my Ph.D. graduation (above).

For Everything there is a Season. In the
ancient Stone Circle at Grange, Lough Gur,
Co. Limerick (top). A.M.E.N. (above).

Augustine's conversion story struck me as being so close to his Irish counterpart, Patrick – the subject of another literary gift that came to enlighten me about the ear of the heart. Fourteen (twice seven – that magical number!) weeks of the summer of 2001 I spent on the St Patrick's Purgatory known as Lough Derg in Co. Donegal. Beavering away on this theology of listening, it was a blessed island to be on. The island, like the ear, never sleeps for these pilgrimage weeks – it is constantly throbbing with prayer, morning, noon and night.

On my first day there, I wandered into the bookshop and emerged an hour later with a little book by Bishop Joseph Duffy called *Patrick in His Own Words*. The sum total of my Patrician experience before this had been in the name of my dear holy father. But the following weeks there I dipped in and out of this saint's story, which is clearly and loudly audiocentric.

The most powerful aural event in it is when Patrick describes a mystical encounter with the Spirit. On one occasion, on being drawn into himself, he not only observed a Spirit presence praying within him, but the Spirit clearly spoke. 'He spoke … saying that he was the Spirit. In this way, [aurally] I learned by experience …'[37] When the eye fails to recognise, the ear hears instantly, obeys and believes.

Patrick's conversion was by ear. He wrote in his own *Confessio* how messages from a Divine Voice crowded into his dreams. One night, when he was tempted by Satan, he frantically shouted out the name of God. The veils of deep depression instantly lifted. 'I believe I was sustained by Christ my Lord and that his Spirit was even then calling out on my behalf.'[38]

37. Duffy, *Patrick in His Own Words*, Veritas, 2000, p. 18.

38. Ibid., p. 17.

This is a powerful sonic statement and event; from the depths of his loud cry, the triune God resounded and saved. Bishop Duffy summarises Patrick's aural and oral prayer thus: 'As the years passed, his prayer grew in intensity. He learned to listen carefully to the promptings of his mind and to see them as coming from God ...'[39] The lesson here for us is to listen carefully and, as St Paul advises, 'pray at all times'.

39. Ibid., p. 63.

Every summer I run workshops for primary school teachers. I truly love the first-hand experience of listening to the classroom adventures of these good people. One such story was around Patrick. This particular schoolteacher had laboured all week to introduce her eight-year-old pupils to the patron saint of Ireland. On the Friday, she asked what had they learned about the Irish saint. One outgoing, friendly lad put up his hand and relayed his understanding of it all: 'Long ago, St Patrick came to Ireland and was told to bring Christy Hannity here from Rome. So he left for Rome in a boat. There he met him and he asked him if he'd like to come to Ireland. He said he would. So St Patrick and Christy Hannity sailed back to Ireland in Patrick's little boat. And that's how Christianity came to Ireland.' A fragment of naive truth here!

There are striking resemblances between our patron saint and the Bishop of Hippo. They lived not only roughly during the same period in history, but were also both founders of the early Christian church. But much more important is the fact that both were spiritually transformed by the sound of God and confessed to this aural ambushing in their own words.

The Emergence of Theosony

UNRAVELLING THE WEB OF MY aural relationship with God, little by little, I welcomed the understanding that my life work was meant to 'obediently' find words for the sound of God. Then, the verb 'to hear' became an act of physical hearing; 'to listen', '*ausculta*', the very first word in the Prologue of St Benedict's Rule, is a divine activity of loving kindness.

I am convinced that my lifelong listening dialogue with the Divine is not, in any manner, exclusive to me, and that such a loving two-way conversation is free to every human being, even the profoundly deaf. How can I say this with such surety? I am merely being faithful to the advice from two different sources: one from the very earliest silent pages of sacred scripture, from the eighth century BC: 'Listen that you may live' (Isaiah 55:3); the second from the twentieth-century Jewish poet, Nelly Sachs, in a poem penned shortly before her death in 1970. Here are some extracts:

> How long have we forgotten how to listen!
> He planted us once to listen ...
> Press, oh press ...
> The listening ear to the earth,

And you will hear, through your sleep
You will hear,
How in death
Life begins.[40]

40. *Women in Praise of the Sacred*, edited by Jane Hirshfield, HarperCollins, 1994, pp. 217, 218.

With the unwanted demise of our marriage, a door opened out to the world of research into the living sound of God. I would probably never have undertaken a Ph.D. if we had not separated. The groaning pain of our relationship was the unwelcomed, yet necessary key that unlocked the research gates. Out of chaos, opportunity brought more than I could ever have wished for. I had a breakthrough moment. The date was 1 February – *Imbolc*, the great Celtic feast of the goddess and Christian saint Brigid; the place was Clare Glens. That was when I heard in the heart's ear a new word which defined the Sound of God, which the fullness of every single sound embodies. The word is 'theosony'.

Clare Glens is a magical nature trail that marks the boundary between the counties of Limerick and Tipperary, and had often been the source of many of our family outings. After midday Mass in Glenstal, my workaday rhythm then was to shelter in this fairytale forest for an hour or so: into the heart of the glens through the level, steady, reliable Limerick walk, out refreshed and renewed down the uneven, unpredictable, surprising Tipperary route. That same afternoon, I tender my gratitude for being 'all ears' to a little canine friend that was with me then: Eve –a six-week old West Highland terrier who found a home with us on the eve of Christmas, 1988, and stayed with us for twelve blessed years. When I could, I took her for

a walk in Clare Glens where she, and I, were really at
ease in our senses: she delighted in nature's smells; I
equally imbibed the aural cosmic sounds all around me
and touched the wise trees in admiration. As her sight
deteriorated, these daily rambles became increasingly
impossible. But I do remember many intimate
moments with her when the sound of my voice filled
that sense of aloneness and challenged her to maintain
her canine instincts as long as she possibly could. From
this little dog, as from that earlier little cocker spaniel
soul friend of mine, Banner, I was saturated with aural
insights.

So that first day of spring of 1999, there we were,
deafened by the sounds all around. Bluebirds, song
sparrows, hermit thrushes and yellow warblers were
the four-part, songbird choir singing their hearts out
overhead in the high trees; water sometimes gurgling
gently as it flowed in an irregular noisy current, sometimes silent at the good of it all, sometimes outdoing all
other sounds as it fell joyfully down the rocks with its
message to 'go with the flow'; the constant murmuring
of the wind whirling proudly through the trees. Here I
was actually in listening awareness, for the first time, it
seemed to me, to the bright Sound of God. The glory of
God was fully alive and well. I was living that world of
change in my life and I was being given the word to
perfectly describe it. *Theosony*.

Theosony is simply a blend of '*Theos*', the Greek for
'God', and '*sonans*', the Latin for 'sounding'. '*Theos*'
identifies the divine miracle that this 'sound' world is;
'*sonans*' challenges us to be ourselves in the 'hear and
now' of that creation, always ready to appear and dis-
appear, always ready to change. The sound of God is

always active, always altering in the sound, never dead or inert and always in the present.

—

Later that year, one normal, or abnormal, October morning, a friend told me about this young, dynamic theologian who was fronting the new theological department in Mary Immaculate College, Limerick. I do not know where the strength came from, but I do remember that it was a particularly painful day in the process of our fading marriage. I rang the college, and the receptionist, Jean, put me through to Dr Eamonn Conway. 'Is this Nóirín Ní Riain, the singer?' he asked. 'Yes – Lord, be merciful to me a singer!' I responded instinctively.

Just as Pilib Ó Laoghaire wholeheartedly and trans-formatively listened thirty years ealier, Eamonn did so a few days later in his new office. I shared all my thoughts and words about God's glorious sounds cap-tured in my up-to-the-minute word 'theosony'. It had not occurred to me to Google the word, but when Eamonn did, we discovered that it had not been claimed. Yes, he would take me on board his new, gleaming theological ship, but I should consider who would act as supervisor. Some Glenstal monks sprang to mind, but I felt, misguidedly, that I couldn't approach anyone in that community as they would merely see or hear me as a female singer.

With a heavy, worried heart that late autumn evening, I returned home, and when I opened the door I was haunted by a fearful lonesomeness. Knowing that the blessed happy days we had shared here in this house as a family were soon to pass, I sensed the voice of God in it all and did what I always do in times of emotional distress. I went up to my little praying room, and in candlelight and fading daylight I sat, prayed and listened. The cosmic sound that kept reverberating was the telephone but I was determined not to be distracted. I awaited the sound of God's voice. Two hours later, I left the room, answered the next call, and it was Eamonn Conway himself. 'I have not supervised anyone yet. But I am willing to oversee your work.' 'This is the day that the Lord has made; let us rejoice and be glad in it' (Psalm 118:24).

Theosony is a new word about an old thing: the phenomenon of listening is ever old, ever new. What theosony does suggest is a lively, vibrant, innovative, perhaps unfamiliar and unusual way of experiencing the loving revelation with the Divine. Theosony has many aural, oral and silent meanings packed into four little syllables. This portmanteau is like divine Esperanto – a concise, one-for-all word for aural prayer. Theosony is a supportive, auxiliary, simple world language that we are all fluent in and can understand throughout the world if we simply listen. Theologian Karl Rahner summarises my understanding of the term 'theosony':

> In every word, the gracious incarnation of God's own abiding Word and so of God himself can take place, and all true hearers of the word are really listening to the inmost depths of every word ... If one is to grow ever more profoundly Christian, one must never cease to practise listening for this incarnational possibility in the human word.[41]

41. Rahner, *Theological Investigations*, Darton, Longman & Todd, 1966, Vol. 4, p. 362.

Explaining Theosony

I. Cosmic Theosony

The universal university of the ear offers a three-level degree course that has no entry requirements except to be human; it is free, and you can take it in your own time, which of course is God's own time.

The first stage guarantees you, just by listening with the ear of the heart, an automatic first-class-honours experience of listening to wordly sounds all around. I called this initial listening step Cosmic Theosony. Our delicate aural sense distinguishes between the extraordinary spectrum of noises; the sound of the gentle breeze is not the sound of the flowing waters. The aural confers a clarity and precision which sight cannot promise.

II. Theosony the Messenger

42. Or 'Kerygmatic Theosony', a lovely little Greek word from theology which in its simplest meaning is something that carries within it a clear message.

The second stage is the Masters degree when you are touched and changed by one particular sound; it carries a message for you either in the words spoken, the memory recalled, the healing sound produced through your own beautiful voice, singing or speaking. It is Theosony as Messenger.[42] That sound reaches the summit through the human voice, which is sacred. The sound of the voice is free. Our voice is freedom, inventiveness of expression and being. Vocal sound is our

most perfect existence. Singers are God's secret yet
sonic agents. But in the silence that follows, God
speaks and there is an answer from God, which is in the
silence that embodies celestial presence.

I had the magnificent blessing of singing Psalm 131 in a Mass setting that Mícheál composed for the centenary celebrations of the Christian Brothers in 1997 alongside the renowned, profoundly deaf percussionist, Evelyn Glennie. We chatted a lot about hearing and silence and she made one remark that sent me the note, the message, I needed then. Not her exact words, but the meaning: that her role was to bring the power of sound to people. In humility, I know that my job is to bring, to sing my own version of the divinity of every sound to people so that they too may experience it. Through an awareness of the sacredness of all sounds, God will be there. It was significant that we should be brought together in this 'psalm of Quiet Trust', the shortest psalm in my treasured Bible. 'But I have calmed and quieted my soul ... Hope in the Lord from this time on and forevermore' (Psalm 131:2, 3).

III. Silent Theosony

The final stage, the doctorate, the Ph.D., the most elusive, mysterious, mystical and most difficult, is when pure sound and silence bring you ear to ear with a Divine/otherworldly presence, which has its own particular name in each tradition. I called it Silent Theosony, borrowing from the very beautiful description of his beloved God by the sixteenth-century mystic, St John of the Cross: 'My beloved ... is silent music'. Everyone can be a doctor in Theosony, the simplest, most accessible doctorate in the world.

169

Lough Gur, home of the most ancient stone circle in Ireland and place of my earliest childhood, taught me a lot about Silent Theosony. One early autumn evening in 2000, I was drawn to revisit this Lough Gur stone circle. The reason revealed itself when I was surprised by two aural insights. First, the deafening din of the sounds of the passing traffic on the busy road between Limerick and Kilmallock. Through the occasional lull came the raucous song of the murder of crows heading home to the rookery. All ecological sounds of the cosmos, the present rhythms of the earth and this listening experience were later to form part of my research to define one classification, one level of listening: cosmic listening.

But there was a more mysterious, miraculous, unseen and unheard power of God in those sacred stones. Standing right in the centre in solitude that evening, the colourful story of Jacob's ladder in scripture came alive and became ahistorical for me:

> Taking one of the stones of the place, he put it under his head and lay down in that place. And he dreamed that there was a ladder set up on the earth, the top of it reaching to heaven; and the angels of God were ascending and descending on it. And the Lord stood beside him and said, '… all the families of the earth shall be blessed in you … Know that I am with you and will keep you wherever you go … for I will not leave you until I have done what I have promised you.' Then Jacob woke from his sleep and said, 'Surely the Lord is in this place – and I did not know it … How awesome is this place! This is none

170

other than the house of God, and this is the gate of heaven.' (Genesis 28:11-17)

Amen! So be it! Jacob, in your own language.

Being in the centre of a *cromlech*, a circle of standing stones, is to know the sound of the silent stone voices. Stones, rocks and pebbles are as audible as they are responsive; the degrees of reception rely on the hearer and the be-holder. A stone is silent because God wants it to be so. Having been conceived beside the oldest stone circle in Ireland, I am at home in this roofless stone house that it forms. To stand at the dead centre of these 113 stones is to be deafened by Silent Theosony. This is the mystical realm of listening and sounding. There is a blurred, yet confident air about it; a silence merged into a sound that redirected my entire being.

Another unexpected wonder of this yet to be named realm of science when the spirit of my singing self could not contain itself was when Mark Patrick Hederman was invited, along with a guest, to attend the Winter Solstice at Newgrange. We arrived for 8.58 a.m., hoping that between then and 9.15 the New-grange chamber would be filled with the light of the rising morning sun and fully aware that, since 1987, only once did the sun shine. This morning too, Father Sun refused to show up. But at one moment, deep inside the cavern I heard a primal sound coming through my throat. I had no conscious awareness of it being a performance. The presence of 'the underworld people', the Tuatha Dé Danann, was here, and although we were in someway gate-crashing their home, they bid us welcome, and this sound, nothing to do with my voice, was a note of gratitude to them for the longstanding

171

protection that they have given and will give in the years ahead. This other force took control and suddenly I was singing in the depth of mound darkness a pre-Christian lament for a dead child, which I had learned years before from the singing of Cáit Ní Ghallchóir. Journalist, Katie Donovan, described it thus one day later in the *Irish Times*: 'Folk and spiritual singer Nóirín Ní Riain, also one of yesterday's visitors, was excited. This was her first time to celebrate it in Newgrange ... Nóirín sang for us a pre-Christian lament of a mother who has lost a child. Her voice filled the chamber, topped with its huge capstone, decorated with its joyful spirals.' My singing was not simply for the megalithic tomb callers, but it had to do with an intuitive sense of memory and belonging to our foreparents, where only vocal sound can lift the veils between these worlds.

Just one other memory of being attuned to Silent Theosony. It was at the liturgical time of Easter Resurrection, 2003. Fr Senan Furlong OSB, plainchant scholar and chanter at Glenstal Abbey, had the great courage to ask me to proclaim the greatest moment of the Easter vigil, to sing the Exultet, traditionally only sung by a male deacon or an ordained man. I was the very first woman to do so in Glenstal Abbey. Although seemingly radical, it was so appropriate, historically and liturgically, since the Risen Christ first appeared to a woman, Mary Magdalen, known by both the Latin and the Greek Eastern Church as '*apostola apostolorum*' – the apostle of apostles. My initial response to his call was negative: how could the sound of my voice ever do justice to the moment. Fear, yet again, threatened to silence a loving freedom to re-imagine myself

172

and my work for God. But Patrick Hederman and Paul Nash, another important Benedictine friend, listened to me before the ceremony and in a silent song without words nodded that there was no choice here. This was God's will, not mine, to be done.

Midnight on Easter Saturday is the Christian high point, the threshold between death and resurrection. I diligently prepared myself to fully enter for the first time my life-long house of belonging to God through singing and listening. At nine o'clock that evening, clutching my score and little Indian drone box, I stole into the Icon Chapel directly underneath the chapel from where I would sing later. Standing before the healing Jesus icon, I brought him in on it and explained all before him, since he was holding up the message promising that 'anyone who is troubled or overburdened should come to me and I will give you rest' (Matthew 11:28). Some cloud of rest and ease calmed me; this was the time of crossing the threshold of doubt and despair into elegance and radiance. All I knew at that moment of reluctance and fear was that this had to be done.

The Easter liturgical scenario was, as always in Glenstal Abbey, beautifully and carefully sculpted: Fr Joseph would incense the lectern, lit only by the wavering flicker of the impressive Paschal candle. Standing behind the nearby pillar, I would, at his discreet nod, approach the lectern and pronounce the Resurrection.

In my physical, rational self, I was unconscious. I wasn't present. I had been anaesthetised. In my nervousness, a silent shroud had fostered a shelter of the love of God wherein I was alone and could stand outside of the world around me. There are different kinds

173

of fear, and moreover, different ways of overcoming this evil, negative force. A form of black-out intoxicated me where I became so much and totally at one with the moment that I was not there at all. It is still a dream I know I have had, but cannot, for the life of me, recall the minute details. Yet I do remember the sight of the flickering Paschal candle, the smell of the pungent incense, the touch of my little drone box, and the faint taste of a throat gargle.

I did come back into consciousness as I turned the final page: singing the 'Amen' is a solid memory that brought me home to myself. I left the lectern and made my way to the back of the crowded church. Blood and soul brothers, Noel and Ciarán, were there and were audibly moved, saying how well I'd done. 'But lads did I sing it all?' I asked. 'I don't remember doing it.'

⁓

The word 'theosony' operates as both noun and adjective; the open ear, the sense of hearing, the world of silence, is the noun. The Psalter favours the noun: 'Sacrifice and offering you do not desire, but you have given me an open ear' (Psalm 40:6).

Then, insofar as theosony ascribes a spiritual characteristic to the human aural sense, it is an adjective. The human race is born of sound and lives by sound. Humanity evolved and sprang into life at the sound of God's call. God is constantly calling out to every human person. The primal sound out of the primal silence can be intimated. It is a sound that is as familiar as it is distant.

With the sensitive support of Abbot Christopher Dillon, I applied to Glenstal Abbey for a hermitage to complete this dissertation. I spent eighteen halcyon

months in Chapel Lake Cottage. In 2003, I was
awarded the first doctorate in theology from Mary
Immaculate College, University of Limerick. Mother
just missed it. She passed over three months earlier, on
20 July at 3 a.m.

Although my appreciation of theosony has a Christian theme, the entire aural cosmic sonata consists of many other themes too. Theosony is all about listening to the Breath of God, which is universal. As the Zen proverb goes: 'Listen to the breath of God. Listen to Muhammad, Jesus and Buddha. But don't get caught up in the name. Listen beyond the names. Listen to the Breath of God.'

No One is Deaf to the Sound of God

EGARDING PHYSICAL DEAFNESS, IT may be asked: is the person deprived of hearing also deprived of religious experience? Of course not; no human being is deaf to the sound of God. In no way is the person divested of hearing, either totally or partially, excluded from the metaphorical, religious, aural, graced experience proposed here. Physical deafness and dumbness do not exclude God's self-revelation. On the contrary. Theosony, the entire range of aural and oral perception of God's self-disclosure, is a metaphor that excludes nobody. Augustine's spiritual deafness was instantly dispelled. '*Ad haec tu dicis mihi, quoniam tu es deus meus et dicis voce forti in aure interiore servo tuo perrumpens meam surditatem.*' (You answered me, for you are my God and your voice can speak aloud in the voice of my spirit, piercing your servant's deafness.)[43] God speaks and is heard in darkness and deafness, through the closed eyes of humanity.

Many people with perfect hearing and perfect pitch choose, and have chosen, to turn deaf ears to God. As the prophet Jeremiah puts it: 'Their ears are closed, they cannot listen.' Not paying attention, closing one's ears to the Word of God, is the ultimate sin of disobedience,

43. Saint Augustine, *The Confessions of Augustine*, edited by Gibb and Montgomery, p. 442.

because as God's voice made flesh clearly states,
'blessed are your ... ears, for they hear' (Matthew 13:16).

God's grace is limitless to all humanity regardless of whether a person hears or speaks. The deaf person ideally fits into the three-way theology of listening: first, through cosmic vibrations, the sound of God is in the ear of the deaf; second, meaningful listening is alive through sign language, an extraordinarily beautiful body language and conversation, which the deaf are quick to point out to us hearers is much more effective, precise and sensitive in communication; and there is the shared space of hearer and non-hearer which is the mystical sound of the Triune God, the ultimate theosony or pure sound of God.

The art of listening, although the most persistent symbol in Hebrew scripture and the New Testament, has been hopelessly neglected in Western theological pursuits. The nature of God is perceived primarily from a visual perspective, largely ignoring the transcendent possibilities of the sense of hearing. The ear is good at playing second fiddle in the theological orchestra.

This is in direct opposition to the contemporary Western truism: 'Actions speak louder than words.' Contemporary Christianity sings ditto; words are only half-alive, the husk is present and correct, but the kernel is lost. The question is how to restore the other half of being human. The answer: restoration is achieved through being able to hear God through 'other' active ears. Martin Luther insisted that 'we must put our eyes into our ears'.

For all of that, over five hundred years later, the eye is still the dominant sense in Western civilization. Not only in Christian theology but in our Western society generally, the work of the ear has sadly been ignored. Somewhere along the line, we were hoodwinked, blindfolded by a world which is almost exclusively visual. We live and speak in an eye's world. The visual forms the speech-coin minted from the imagination. Whatever way you 'look' at it, we inhabit an eye-centric world. 'I see' says it all when we listen well to the other; 'd'you see what I mean' amplifies and is the full stop on any personal point of view. The irony is that these two verbal divining rods reside in the ear because, as in all spoken phrases, they are heard, first and foremost, in the inner ear of the speaker, and then in the outer ear of the listener. But as Gaston Bachelard summarises: 'Sight *says* too many things at one time. Being does not see itself ... it *listens* to itself.'[44]

44. Bachelard,
*The Poetics of
Space*, Beacon
Press, 1994,
p. 215; italics
mine.

We all have experienced the beyond-belief place that the eye holds in human relationship. When we love, it is through our eyes that we silently pierce and dredge the heart of the other. The loved one desires the look of the lover and calls forth a response. Through the glance, we learn all too quickly whether we are loved, respected, appreciated. 'Keep your eyes open', 'look out' we constantly advise our young ones. The eyes provide many of our inmost secrets – joy, pain, disdain, ingratitude, encouragement and discouragement.

But the ear is our intuitive life-sound metal detector. We live a life of being 'all ears' to another. An aural, sensual understanding forms the very fabric of all our imaginations if we can but *obediently* listen. We say, 'I give you my word'; 'I can say no more'. There is the little phrase 'Mum's the word', which has to do, I had always boasted, with a mother's natural innate discretion about secrets. But recently I received an email from a friend, who knows my obsessions with sound and silence, about the origin of this informal motto. 'Mum' is all to do with sound and silence; it is the mimicking of the sound sharply closing one's lips makes because of unwillingness to add any further comment. Thus 'mum's the word' means 'mum's the silence' too.

Such neglect of the aural affects the spiritual climate also. According to Søren Kierkegaard, the ear 'is the most spiritually determined of the senses'.[45] Favouring the visual and the visible in all areas of life has, in the words of Joachim Ernst Berendt, generally 'despiritualised our existence'.[46]

Hearing, Berendt concurs with Kierkegaard, 'is none the less the most spiritual of all our senses'.[47] Through learning and practising hearing, not only is one's quality of life enhanced but God's self-revelation is more readily and obediently received.

If we, as clergy and laity, women and men, in Ireland were able to listen kindly, openly and respectfully to one another, would we be in this same state of alienation, emptiness, distrust and despairing pain? Not one of us would listen to the little lost souls of horrific abuse, not one of us would listen to the onlookers, not one of us would listen to the ill perpetrators to offer them a healing hand. 'How long, you people, shall my honour suffer shame? How long will you love vain words, and seek after lies' (Psalm 4:2).

Theological scholarship has also ignored any serious discussion of silence. I could not believe at this time of theosony research that of the sixteen major reference sources I looked up, only *seven* contained any specific reference to silence.

45. Kierkegaard, *Either/Or*, translated by David F. Swenson/ Lilian Marvin Swenson, Princeton University Press, 1944 (1959), Vol. 1, p. 66.

46. Berendt, *The Third Ear*, Henry Holt & Co., 1992, p. 23.

47. Ibid., p. 24.

Medical advancements in the area of the aural lag behind the visual. The first *British Journal of Medicine* devoted to the sense of hearing did not appear until 2002. There have been considerable advances in relation to the doctoring of the eye. The cornea of the eye can be reshaped and adjusted by laser treatment or refractive surgery to enhance sight. At least 90 per cent of vision can be restored twenty-four hours after this procedure. The failing ear has still to rely on mechanical hearing aids.

As I took up the exciting challenge of expressing my own aural/Divine relationship, I also 'looked at' the biology of the ear. What a marvellous little apparatus it is, the most sophisticated and sensitive sense in interpreting and understanding the outer physical world.

The ear has a miraculous ability to receive information from the world without and within the body itself, above and beyond any other physical sense. The most thrilling service of the ear is to deliver us from aloneness, to be the little instrument which lets us hear the sound of ourselves and of one another, to share our inmost thoughts, to understand one another through the voice.

The human body can discern sounds beyond the audible through sound vibrations that penetrate the very walls of the physical body. The body is, in this sense, an extension of the ear. The first attachment and connection to the world is through the ear in the womb. The eye is not a comparable extension or as attuned to the reception of the world around.

The ear hears in both light and darkness; the eye cannot behold the external world in darkness. One hears differently in the dark; to listen deeply and thoughtfully is enhanced when one closes one's eyes.

Whereas the eye ceases to be effective when it enters alienating atmospheres like fog or darkness, the ear continues to function in every situation and all through the night.

Within the ear resides the seat of emotion. It can be a transcendental medium. Religion is an emotional relationship with God. Religious emotion that is excited by the contemplation of God is called 'Theopathy'. At the thought of God, the ear tingles.

For survival, the brain relies upon three main sources of energy: food, air and energy from our senses. The aural sense provides most of this third source of energy to the brain. This is why the ear is an insomniac. It never sleeps. It dare not, because it is constantly providing and supplying energy to that seat of thought, memory and emotion. According to the French Canadian physician, Dr Alfred Tomatis, 'the ear provides the nervous system with almost 90 per cent of its overall sense energy'.[48]

48. Tomatis, *The Conscious Ear*, Station Hill Press, 1991, p. 186.

As regards other interesting facts about the ear: sense of balance resides in the ear – essential to a state of rest which is equilibrium, vital to the attainment of inner peace. The frequency range of hearing is ten times greater than that of sight. The ear has a much greater range of sensitivity.

Colours cannot be seen in different frequencies but sound can be heard in limitless frequencies. In the light spectrum, there is a series of seven colours: red, orange, yellow, green, blue, indigo and violet. These are produced when white light, such as sunlight, is passed through a prism which decomposes into rays of different colour and wavelength. For instance, the rays of longest wavelength produce the colour red, the shortest produce violet. Although these seven colours can be perceived in varying degrees of colour between the primary colours themselves, they can only be looked at in one frequency, as it were. The point is more readily understood when compared with a sound analogy. For example, in Western classical music, there are seven notes in the musical scale. However, these notes can be heard in higher and lower frequencies. Take, for instance, the note known as 'middle C' at the centre of the piano keyboard. This note can be heard at higher and lower frequencies depending on the amount of octaves on that particular keyboard. There is only one octave of colour perception.

The ear was constructed by the Creator with such biological complexity, such physiological ingenuity, that it can go way beyond itself in its operational capacity as a purely sensory organ. Even these scientific and biological facts are a revelation.

But what about the voice? Deep within the larynx or voice-box are two pairs of vocal chords: the upper fold, called false vocal chords, are the silent ones and are redundant in the production of vocal sound; the lower true vocal chords are the vital, noisy folds, vibrating, making sound when air from the lungs breezes through. Sounds from the larynx then proceed to the organ on the floor of the mouth, the tongue. There is a direct line from the throat, the larynx, to the inner, middle ear, which in turn runs on to the mind/brain. As a result, bodily sounds do not have to leave the body to be heard. No one else can ever hear the true sound of your own voice. In other words, feedback takes place from the brain to the inner ear; a part of the sound returns from the brain to the cochlea. Every spoken sound is heard in the ear. The larynx cannot keep secrets from the ear. The voice and the ear are one; they are simply two sides of the one coin. Your human voice contains sounds that only you can hear. The aural dictates the parameters of the oral. There is no personal orality without the aural. No other person can hear precisely these head sounds. In other words, once the sound of the human voice leaves the body to communicate to the world around, the sound changes.

Until I understood this connection between voice and brain, I was always disturbed at any recording of my own voice. I still find it disconcerting when I listen back to my recordings. I cringe at the spoken snippet on my answering machine message and react: 'Surely, that's not me!' And it isn't! No one hears your true voice, the passport to your soul. Only God hears the pure drop of every single creature.

The Last Word
on the Ear of the Heart

YOU NOW HAVE HEARD SOME adventures of growth and wisdom for me through my personal story. Of course I had to be strict and could not tell it all. So I discerned carefully what were the moments in my life when the grace of the ear allowed the electricity and eccentricity of divine energy to percolate through, when the ear was a natural acoustic chamber where the voice of God resounds, almost like that Mount Marian seashell echoing the eternal sounds of the ocean.

I now live in a little hermitage in the shadow of the monastery of Glenstal Abbey. My heart is at home and safe here and I love the life of praying with the community, morning, noon and night. Strangely, after this almost constant seven-year cycle of attending the daily prayer-stops of Matins, Lauds, the Eucharist, Vespers and Compline, when I am out in the world, I intuitively, unconsciously 'tune in' at these five prayer times and can be found praying aloud from the lovely little Glenstal Prayer Book, on whose editorial board I was blessed to be the only lay member.

Some delightful days and nights over the past few years have been spent singing with Eoin and Moley. AMEN is our collective name, which again, like theosony before it, surprised me one day when we were driving in the car to sing at a wedding of a handsome couple.

AMEN is an acronym: A. stands for the audience, the Almighty, the Absolute or simply anybody; M. is for Moley; E. stands for Eoin; and N. for yours truly. I have learned how to really be myself without fear through singing with my two sons. There is something so special about the way it unfurled of its own accord and it has been a very rich and smooth bridge over the troubled waters which a life of singing has sometimes been. A gift from God. May that same God continue to bless this theosonic family and its listeners! Amen! So be it! (Incidentally, as well as complementing one another vocally, we are each one of us happy being together: Eoin, the pragmatic one, drives, keeps the business folders and negotiates the fees! Moley is the trickster who keeps us amused with funny tales, faces, stange sounds and quirky news stories from the papers. All the while, I am happily in the back, saying the Rosary!)

The truth of divine sound is not confirmed until it changes the religious experience in attunement with the true potential of human hearing. Initially, the listening is false because theosony, the sound of God, is actually hidden and drowned out by the everyday sound of living. Discerning the aural distractions that deflect one's attention to theosony is the theological application of being 'all ears'. In this obedient theosony, the listening ear becomes an organ of religious experience, religious being. Seamus Heaney takes up the anthem:

49. Heaney,
'Station Island',
Station Island,
p. 90.

Hear it calling out to every creature ... the collect of a new epiphany ... it's time to swim out on your own and fill the element with signatures on your own frequency ...[49]

It has been the intention of this book to flesh out, through one human sense, the wider, more personal picture of prayer. The listening adventure with God is *anam saothair* (soul work), characterised by a close and warm relationship, which is deeply personal, sometimes painful and even secret.

My own most cherished, simple relationship with God has, now you know, been aural. Confidence in the prayerful power of sound reflects my own life's pilgrimage. Being and waiting in silence has always jolted and permitted me to pray. A great German twentieth-century writer, Max Picard, who wrote a classic book on silence, *The World of Silence*, summarises it perfectly:

50. Picard, *The World of Silence*, Gateway Edition, 1951, p. 33.

When you are silent, you are like someone awaiting the creation of language for the first time ... In the silence, you are ready to give the word back to the Creator from whom you first received it. Therefore, there is something holy in almost every silence.[50]

Singing, praying, hearing, sounding and silence all come from the same source for me. When I am in deepest song, my ordinary consciousness transforms into one harmonious sound in which I live and move and am. I am transported into a world of sound which is real and not contrived. My body is an aural sound board of God, a 'Temple of the Holy Spirit' in direct response to the voice of God – a human resonating chamber for the Divine. Kahlil Gibran made this observation: 'Your body is the harp of your soul, And it is yours to bring forth sweet music …'[51]

God is the sound engineer who fine-tunes the organic spiritual melody of each one of us, modifying it to create the most perfect sound of love. So I can hear myself in the raw, naive, subjective listening. Then God edits and doctors the sound until it is the frequency which allows me and you to hear the call. My life is a crusade of the sound and the sacred – a mission of pray-sing towards praising.

I wanted to put words on a simple human obedient listening to the God who listens as intently to us as the Divine One listened to that one incarnate logos of the Easter Christ-story. This is the ultimate theosony – penetratingly embodied by the Welsh parson poet R.S. Thomas in the final stanza of a poem entitled 'The Musician':

So it must have been on Calvary
In the fiercer light of the thorns' halo:
The men standing by and that one figure,
The hands bleeding, the mind bruised but calm,
Making such music as lives still.
And no one daring to interrupt
Because it was himself that he played
And closer than all of them the God listened.[52]

Thank you for listening,

51. Gibran, The Prophet, A.A. Knopf, 1923, p. 72.

52. Thomas, 'The Musician', The Faber Book of Religious Verse, edited by Helen Gardner, Faber and Faber, 1972, p. 337.

Acknowledgements

Marion, my dearest sister, and her husband, Dr Stephen Flynn, have always minded me spiritually and physically, and their wonderful family are always there for me too. Without my kind-hearted brother, Noel, I could never have stumbled through separation and divorce. Annette was a strong power behind him through it all. The Ryan dynasty is a great blessing in my life.

Mícheál Ó Súilleabháin is someone who will always hold a special place in my heart and I am so grateful to him for all the reasons that he knows in the secrets of his own heart.

Our two lads, Eoini and Moley – what can I say! Two fine sons, in whom I am not just well, but magnificently pleased. Thank you, Size 2 Shoes, for standing tall with me.

I tender my gratitude to all at Veritas Publications, particularly Donna Doherty, whose idea it was from the start, Caitríona Clarke, Lir Mac Cárthaigh, and Amanda and Ruth too.

This text, let alone a Ph.D., would never have seen the light of day without the presence of Dr Eamonn Conway, my supervisor, for the three years of my doctoral research. Your courage to take this outsider under your wing was truly remarkable.

The extremely generous input and the editing of three people during those research years were invaluable: Abbot Patrick Hederman OSB, the late John O'Donohue and Br Cyprian Love OSB. Br Colmán was the patient librarian throughout.

Four of the five Abbots of the Benedictine community of Glenstal Abbey have warmly welcomed me and opened various doors physically and spiritually. We never met the first Abbot, Joseph Dowdall, who passed over in 1966. The late Abbot Augustine O'Sullivan openly embraced the novel, courageous venture of embarking on a recording with us in the late 1970s. (He even hosted a simple champagne reception for us all after Midnight Mass, Christmas 1979, on the launch of *Caoineadh na Maighdine*. He had a wonderful sense of the feminine, and his devotion to *Muire, Máthair Dé*, Mary, the Mother of God, still continues to inspire me.) Then the gracious Abbot Celestine Cullen blessed both a residency for Mícheál, Eoin and myself in Glenstal Abbey in 1982, and the next two recordings that we were to make. I will always be so grateful to Abbot Christopher Dillon who twice listened to my genuine *cri de coeur*, and persisted until the community heard and responded to allow me a residency here in Glenstal Abbey from which to pray, sing, work and live. Before he was ever elected fifth Abbot of this monastery in 2008, Patrick Hederman and I were united in a friendship built on the shared trust in that subtle yet sure presence of the Holy Spirit in all that we do and say. Prayer, this mystic Abbot teaches, is simply about 'being attuned to the tempo, the texture and the idiom of God's way of relating to us'.[53]

Then the Benedictine community of the monastery at large – over the years, you all have been so treasured by me and each one of you is a story in my heart.

53. Hederman, *The Furrow*, March 2001, p. 131.

190

Ciarán Forbes OSB has been and will forever be a life-
long personal and family friend. Gregory Collins is a
beautiful monastic genius, whose love and prayers I
cherish daily. Last but not least in this Glenstal litany is
Marmion, the eccentric monastery cat, who stridently
purred me on to the finishing line!

Hilary Fennell, Íde Ní Laoghaire and Fanny Howe
were challenging, passionate, yet always encouraging
and supportive readers at an early stage. I also salute
long-term friends, Dolores Whelan, Marie Richardson
and Jean Fitzgerald; Anne Harris, an angel whose
friendship is a beautiful treasure, Aengus Fanning and
all the *Sunday Independent* family; Sr Una Agnew SSL
and all the St Louis sisters; Dr Patricia Kiernan; poet
David Whyte; Elinore Detiger; musician, Paul Winter,
his beautiful wife Chez and all the Winter Consort
who were my Solstice friends for eight years at the
Cathedral of St John the Divine in New York and also
on many fun-filled tours; my Lough Derg family,
Monsignor Richard Mohan, Deborah Maxwell, Mary
McDaid and Fr Lawrence Flynn; Abbess Marie and
my Cistercian sister-friends of St Mary's Abbey,
Glencairn, (you know, sisters, how I not only beg for
your prayers, I depend upon them!); Pat Donnellan
and all at Annaghmakerrig; my legendary and gener-
ous cousin, Pat Delaney; Declan Casey; Peter and
Trudy Ferguson; Anne O'Leary; Margaret Denton-
Daly; Leonard Appel and Marie Milis of Initiations,
Belgium; Richard Kearney; John Masterson; John
Dunford; Robbi McMillan; Mary Condren; Norman
Winter; Margaret McDonnell; and Fr Michael Wall.

In memoriam of John O'Donohue, who passed
over too early for me to really say thank you for all he did

for me; Dermot Patrick Sheridan, a lad called back in flight at the age of twenty-four; and my parents, Nora and Paddy Ryan.

My final acknowledgement of gratitude rests with the triune God. The All-powerful Trinity created us human beings to pray constantly and my life, particularly in its inevitable darknesses and doubts, has been a prayer spiralling up to the Divine like incense. As the Scots-Gallic wild axiom puts it: a big prayer, a little prayer, I send to you in space. Arrange them yourself, O God of Grace!

Christ taught humanity how to listen and pray in human words. The Holy Spirit guided and enlightened the 'pen of the scribe' in so many mysterious ways that one could never forget that 'He who planted the ear, does he not hear?' (Psalm 94:9.)

Benedicamus Domino. Deo Gratias.
Let us bless the Lord. Thanks be to God.

Discography & Bibliography

Recordings

1978 *Seinn Aililiú*, Gael Linn.

1980 *Caoineadh na Maighdine*, Gael Linn.

1982 *Good People All (The Darkest Midnight)*,
Glenstal Records.

1988 *Stór Amhrán (Songs learned from Pilib
Ó Laoghaire)*, The Mercier Press (reprinted
2007, Ossian Publications).

1989 *Vox de Nube*, Gael Linn.

1990 *Nóirín Ní Riain with the Monks of Glenstal
Abbey*, CBS Records.

1993 *Soundings, Spiritual Songs from Many Traditions*,
Ossian Publications.

1996 *River of Stars*, Sounds True Inc.

1996 *Celtic Soul*, Earth Music Productions.

1997 *Gregorian Chant Experience*, The O'Brien Press
Ltd.

2004 *Mystical Ireland (The Virgin's Lament, Darkest
Midnight and Vox de Nube)*, Sounds True Inc.

2004 *Biscantorat: Sound of the Spirit from Glenstal
Abbey* DVD & CD, with Sinéad O'Connor and
John O'Donohue, Hummingbird.

2007 *A.M.E.N.*, with sons Eoin and Micheál P.
Ó Súilleabháin, The Daisy Label.

2008 *Celtic Joy*: US release of *A.M.E.N.*, Sounds True
Inc.

COMPILATIONS AND GUEST RECORDINGS

1977 *Óró Damhnaigh*, produced by Mícheál Ó Súilleabháin, Gael Linn.

1984 *James Last at St Patrick's Cathedral, Dublin*,
Polydor.

1992 *Solstice Live at the Cathedral of St John the
Divine, New York*, Earth Music Productions.

1994 *Sieben Psalmen with Markus and Simon
Stockhausen*, EMI Classics.

1996 *Lumen, European Song Contest*, Virgin Records.

1996 *Native Wisdom: World Music of the Spirit*,
Narada.

1997 *Illumination, Hildegard von Bingen*, produced by
Richard Souther, Sony.

1997 *Agnes Browne*, Anjelica Huston, Hell's
Kitchen/October Films (soundtrack).

1997 *Anthology of Sacred World Music, Vol. 1*, Sounds
True.

2001 *In deiner Nähe, Close to You*, produced by Markus
Stockhausen, Aktivraum.

2008 *Sanctuary*, various artists, Independent.

—

PRODUCER/MUSICAL DIRECTOR

2004 *Biscantorat*, Hummingbird Records.

2007 *A.M.E.N.*, Daisy Label/Sounds True.

2007 *In Praise of Mary, the Cistercian Nuns of St
Mary's Abbey, Glencairn, Co. Waterford*, The
Daisy Label.

—

BIBLIOGRAPHY

1985 'The Female Song in the Irish Tradition' in *Irish
Women, Image and Achievement* (edited by Eiléan
Ní Chuileanáin), Arlen House, pp. 73–84.

1987 *Ím Bím Baboró, Rabhcáin do Leanaí, Children's Songs from the Irish Tradition*, The Mercier Press.

1988 *Stór Amhrán, A Wealth of Songs from the Irish Tradition*, Ossian Publications. Reprinted 2007.

1993 'The Nature and Classification of Traditional Religious Songs in Irish with a Survey of Printed and Oral Sources' in *Music in the Church* (edited by Gerard Gillen and Harry White), Irish Academic Press.

1997 *Gregorian Chant Experience*, The O'Brien Press Ltd.

1998 *Sacred Moments*, Valerie O'Sullivan, Veritas, pp. 94–7.

1999 *The Whoseday Book*, The Irish Hospice Foundation.

1999 'Digging for Sound in the Celtic Tradition' in *Celtic Threads* (edited by Pádraigín Clancy), Veritas.

2001 'The Sound of God' in *Anáil Dé – The Breath of God* (edited by Helen Phelan), Veritas, pp. 177–89.

2005 'Towards a Theology of Listening' in *Spirituality*, Vol. 2, No. 62, pp. 286–90, Dominican Publications.

2006 'Bringing It All Back Home: The Retrieval of Gregorian/Plainchant and the Forgotten Sense in *Time [to] Change* (edited by Joseph Putti), Veritas, pp. 170–86.

2009 'The Ear of the Heart: Weaving a Tapestry of Transformative Listening in Song and Story' in *Intimacy – Venturing the Uncertainties of the Heart*, Jungian Odyssey Series Vol. 1, Spring Journal, Louisiana, USA, pp. 9–17.

INDEX